Sunderland

Memories

Sunderland

Memories

Living History (North East)

First published in 2008 by
The History Press
The Mill, Brimscombe Port,
Stroud, Gloucestershire, GL5 2QG
www.thehistorypress.co.uk

Reprinted in 2009

British Library Cataloguing in Publication Data.
A catalogue record for this book is available from the British Library.

ISBN 978 0 7524 4491 8

Typesetting and origination by
The History Press
Printed in Great Britain

Contents

Acknowledgements

Living History (North East) must acknowledge the contribution made by the Friends and Volunteers of Oral History (FAVOH) and its great debt of gratitude to many people for being involved in the research and editing of this book. A list of those people whose recollections have been drawn upon is appended. Many people made contributions but not all could be included in this one publication. The volunteers who are the backbone of LHNE are also listed. Especial thanks are owed to Stuart Miller, Sylvia Thompson, Carol Bell and John Brantingham who became involved in the later stages and who contributed many photographs.

Introduction

The extracts which follow are derived from the memories, (tape/video-recorded or written), of a range of people who were born in, or lived in Sunderland during the last century. The bulk of them are from the 1930s onward, although a few precede that. In other words the extracts do not provide an image of life in Sunderland at a precise time, but over a period from the 1930s to the 1980s. They give a wide coverage of experiences and perceptions and are the recollections of people drawn from a wide range of social and economic backgrounds, though it would be impossible in a book of this size to offer any more than a sample of reminiscences. Indeed the extracts themselves are, as will be obvious, simply brief extracts taken from much more substantial accounts.

The organisation of the extracts under the headings, 'Childhood', 'Home and Lifestyle', 'Leisure', 'Church', 'Schooldays', 'Wartime' and 'Working', follows the main stages of life, but did mean that some arbitrary choices about positioning had to be made on occasion. 'Home and Lifestyle' is a very general section, but then so much of life is! 'Wartime' is almost wholly concerned with the Second World War, but of course Wearside people were involved in many other conflicts which do not figure here. It is also mainly concerned with the home front rather than active service overseas since this book is primarily about Wearside life. 'Working' encompasses a variety of occupations and employment, but cannot pretend to be comprehensive. Many accounts covered the whole range of experiences or at least several of them; therefore the same people appear sometimes more than once within different categories. In very many cases what is presented is a very small proportion of the whole, and large sections were unused for the purpose of this book. As well as the people who are represented in here there were many other accounts which do not appear here at all; these were also taken out mainly because of duplication, or because there were rather better stories about the same theme. Hopefully at some time in the future it may be possible to include some of the unused material in another book of this type.

Many of these stories are taken from live recordings of memories made by trained volunteers working for Living History (North East) (LHNE). This organisation is described below. Transcriptions of those recordings were the basis for the chosen sections. Inevitably it is difficult to capture the actual dialect and tone of the person. In fact, non-Wearsiders would have had some difficulty in interpreting some of the quite distinctive language used in this area, quite apart from the accent, so these sections have been largely 'sanitised' for the purpose. Many of the stories told here are about very sad and traumatic experiences and this is not easily captured fully in written extracts. There is also, though, a common tendency to make light of difficulties and, with the benefit of hindsight, to enhance the 'golden age' aspects of the past. This is a frequent issue in evaluating oral reminiscences.

Nevertheless the inescapable image which is presented is one of personal resilience and courage, 'making the most of things', strong family lives, social cohesion and working discipline. Of course these qualities, however reliant on self-selecting memories, were based upon circumstances which have disappeared. The decimation of heavy industry on Wearside since the 1980s, the revolution in information and communications technology, (which has had all sorts of implications), a general rise in the standard of living and much more comprehensive state support, to name but a few factors, mean that this is a past which could not be restored and is perhaps better left in a 'golden age'. However, the personal qualities and social standards associated with it are timeless ones which can be maintained partly by means of the process of oral transmission.

The illustrations which have been used also originate from a diversity of sources. Some are in the possession of LHNE. Others are used here by kind permission of other archival organisations or individuals. A good number of them were associated specifically with particular individual reminiscences. Others are contextual rather then specific. Of course these are photographs which have survived a long process of attrition and selection so it cannot be claimed that they are comprehensive or necessarily typical of life. Inevitably, as is the way of things with photographs, many of them were never associated with full captions although the general theme is clear enough.

Nowadays there is much greater emphasis upon the importance of oral history as a historical source, particularly about the lives of ordinary people. Modern techniques, training and equipment mean that coverage is much more comprehensive and sensitive. As the pace of change hastens there is far greater awareness of the need to capture memories of the nearer past before they disappear. In the forefront of changing attitudes to the role of oral history are many voluntary organisations such as Living History (North East).

LHNE was formally established in 1995, when a number of passionate enthusiasts became increasingly aware of the void in recorded memory, not just in Sunderland but across the region. There was a great sense of urgency as we approached a new millennium that the social, economic, political and environmental climate had changed considerably. Sunderland had lost its heavy industries all at once and there were very few historical footnotes to the thousands of men and women who had spent their lives working in or alongside mining, shipbuilding and construction. It was this sense of 'injustice' in historical materials that initiated the creation of LHNE. From those early formative days we have continued in our pursuit to place the collection and documentation of oral history within the region on the map. Consequently, in 2007 LHNE opened the region's first oral history centre to reflect the unique cultural heritage of the North East.

one

Childhood

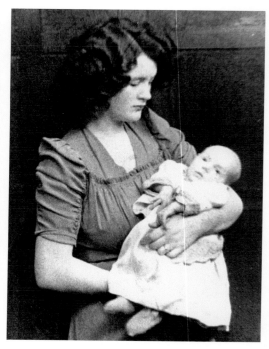

A young child ready to play in the street with her ball.

Winnie Davis with her first child. Winnie is a prominent community activist who was awarded the MBE.

Sans Street, looking east from Coronation Street corner, 1935.

We would play in the street

In the 1930s I lived in Sans Street…We would play in the street but kept to your own street as much as you could. If we could borrow a roller skate we would play in Suffolk Street as Sans Street had cobbles… If we went any distance at all we would go to Tunstall Hill and pinch turnips, 'nashers' we called them. West Park where there were roundabouts and swings or to Mowbray Park to feed the ducks: there was always a hoard of kids. We would push a pram with one at the top and one at the bottom. We would take a bottle of what we called Spanish Water, we would buy liquorice and shake it up in the bottle of water and bread and marga-rine wrapped in newspaper; that was the bait. Sometimes we played under the gaslights.

W.D.

I was about ten when I made my first bogey

I was about ten when I made my first bogey using two sets of pram wheels, a plank with back wheels fixed, the front made to swivel by means of a nut and bolt, the hole made with a hot poker. Many hours of fun making and playing with my bogey.

B.C.

What days we had up on Cage Hill

What days we had up on Cage Hill, because it was a bank, and if you had your sledge, we used to have a good time going down Cage Hill. To make the sledge you would get a penny worth of irons from Catty Allen's.

J.C.

Oh, how I wish I could return

Oh, how I wish I could return and have a full tin of polish to play itchy. Mine never sounded the same, as only an empty tin or half full was allowed as my grand-da polished everyone's shoes every night (that was important – clean shoes!) I never had to wait long for a tin… My treasures were cherub scraps, nearly a full set, stilts made from baked-bean tins, with string being on the tubby side, I used to flatten one or the other, a leather casey… and my alleys (marbles) with the best in a box.

O.H.

Putta der gun down

I was brought up in Southwick, affectionately known locally as 'Suddick', which is located on the north bank of the river Wear at Sunderland. In the mid-1950s I was educated at High Southwick Junior School and well remember the history lessons, in which we learnt about the Battle of Hastings, fought in 1066, the War of the Roses and the numerous skirmishes involving the Scots at Bannockburn, Culloden, etc. Those lessons were usually the prelude to our own battles… We usually split into two groups, with one being the 'goodies' and the other group the 'baddies'. Battle would usually commence on the order of a leader and the duration would usually be until your mam called you in for your next meal, or until one side was wiped out. We did not have real bows and arrows, we merely mimicked the actions of a bowman, but the accuracy of the arrows was better than the real thing, with a 'hit' every time. However, members of the opposite team would usually dispute that you had hit them and they would not play 'dead'. It was usually in close combat that you were able to convince them that you had 'killed' them, after running them through with your invisible sword. We did not need medical assistance in those days, as all that it took to bring you back to life was a 'tig' or touch from someone on your own team and you were alive again and free to continue, fully armed and invincible. Participants of these games were multi-lingual and could speak every language on the planet. For example, the German side could speak fluent German, such as 'Putta der gun down' or 'Donner und blitzen I have been kilt'…

J.B.

So began open warfare

In the winter of 1947, when I was ten years old and lived in the area of Hendon, we were sent home from school in the morning because of a snow blizzard; it was so bad I walked straight past my street and it was not until I came to the fish and chip shop that I realised what I had done. At this time when it snowed everyone cleared their part of the pavement, also when the snow got too heavy for the roof of the house it slid down like a mini-avalanche, consequently the snow piled high in the gutter and spilled out into the road. We, the children, started making snow blocks and built an igloo with no roof. It was so cold it did not melt so lasted for about a week. Other children further down the street, on seeing what we had made, then copied and so began open warfare raiding each other's igloos trying to destroy them and there was also the job of keeping a supply of snow balls at the ready.

D.L.

Sometimes we went to the beach to play

Sum o' the games I remember are ones we played in the street because there wasn't much room inside the 'ouse and nothing to do 'cept maybe read! We had loads o' friends and loads of fun playin' out all hours; tops and whips; marbles; jumpy-on-back; mounty Kitty; jack-shine-the-maggy [hide and seek with a torch in the dark]; in and out those dusty bluebells; 'Aah wrote a letter to my love and on the way I lost it; bobby bingo; hide and seek; duck stone; kick the can; bowling hoops; knocky nine doors; tally ho; hitchy coit [hopscotch]; french cricket; rounders. Sometimes we went to the beach to play. We had to walk unless we had the fare for a tram ride. Our mams used ter knit our cossies and when they got wet they used t' hold the watter and pull down to our bums!

Anon.

Do you remember getting small frogs

Do you remember getting small frogs from Boldon Flats Pond? We used to get a 3d return ticket to East Boldon and collect frogs by the hundreds in blue Ostermilk tins. Mine was always blue, but if your family had money they would be yellow, talk about class distinction – there was not many yellow ones, if any, in the area where we lived. Me and John Bonnelli from Norman Street used to make parachutes using hankie thread tied at the four corners and harness them to the frogs then launch them from the window sill. We were only about six then. I know it's cruel but we were only very young and did not realise they were not commandos. Peter Someo's ice cream – now that was some ice cream, he was out all weathers selling his Tappieeeeee Appleeeeees (that was his Italian cry as he made his way around the streets of Hendon selling his ice cream). His nose used to dribble in the winter months and drop into the ice-cream barrel, maybe that's where the nice flavour of his ice cream came from.

N.P.

The games I can remember

During the war years and after, we could not buy sweets or fruit. All we used to buy was liquorice root, black Spanish and one penny oxo. The chocolate machines were all taken away. Toys were hard to come by. My dad, being a shipwright, was good at woodwork.

So he made a doll's house, furniture, tanks, guns, airplanes. He made a ship with a mouse-trap inside and when you rolled a little iron ball along the floor it pushed the button on the side of the ship and it blew up. The games I can remember were top and whip, a game with cardboard milk tops, train tickets, skipping ropes, (double Dutch), glass marbles, hide and seek, the big ships sailed through the ally-ally-o, roller skates, catchy-kiss, chuck stones.

M.T.

The 'Sunshine Corner' song

How well I remember those hot days on Roker beach when I was a small child. Sitting on the warm sand listening to the stories told to a crowd of kids at the 'Sunshine Corner'. I don't remember the stories now but I remember the singing. We started off with the 'Sunshine Corner Song', which went:

> *Sunshine Corner is the place for me,*
> *For all good children under ninety-three.*
> *All are welcome, seats are given free.*
> *Roker Sunshine Corner is the place for me!*

The tune was catchy and was sung with gusto by all the children who flocked to the meeting. It was one place mothers could leave their children for a while knowing they would be safe.

D.G.

Roker Beach in the 1920s.

It was lovely golden sand

My dad took me to catch whiting fish. At that time, before the Second World War, the fish used to come inshore very close and the fishermen were able to cast in from the beach to catch them, they were so numerous – they practically gave themselves up. It was a chance to get some cheap fish. This happened at the beach near where I lived at Ryhope. I can vaguely remember being told to sit away from the shoreline and watch the floats and bait while they caught the fish. It was late at night in the summer and moonlight. It seemed a great adventure at the time, I suppose I would only be six to seven years old. My dad was a miner, I don't think he was a keen fisherman, but it was a chance to get some cheap fish and also enjoy the lovely night and the fresh air, which was precious to a man working in the dark underground, amongst the dust and heat.

S.H.

I remember a trip to Roker

I remember a trip to Roker during the early 1930s. Mam and the ladies settled on the beach, the dads took us to Roker Park to see the model boats on the lake. The weather was ideal for sailing little yachts. Wandering round the lake, my younger brother Fred and I were so engrossed in the small regatta scudding across the lake that our ice creams melted. Turning to ask dad a question I found he had disappeared with the other men. I decided we should find our way back to mam on the beach. Finding the park entrance then the beach we headed the way we had come. Trudging through the sand, legs getting more tired, Fred started to cry. A lady, on seeing our distress, took our hands and walked along the beach with us. A few yards on we came upon our group of mams who were quite unaware we had even been lost.

B.G.

Buckley family and friends on the beach at Seaburn.

In the Wizard's Bath

Sometimes we went down the beach at Seaburn and played in the Wizard's Bath. This was a long, narrow, shallow hollow in the rocks beside the prom, where water remained when the tide went out. We would fish with a bent pin and a length of black cotton to catch tiddlers we took home, but being so small we didn't keep them and even the cat wouldn't eat them.

P.S.

A bit pork was a treat

We used t'gerra penny a week pocket money. We cud buy penny scented cachous or a couple o' hard black likrish sticks or locusts or brown likrish root t'chew or two bull's eyes. At Christmas wi hung ower stockins on the brass rail ower the fireplace. Me brothers gorran engine an' a train set. I gorra little dolly. The' might be a selection box or a few sweets, an apple an' an orange, an' that was it! For Christmas dinner we might gerra chop or sum ham – a bit pork was a treat.

Anon.

It was a jam jar entrance

My brothers used to go from Easington Lane to the Imperial Cinema, known as the Imp, in Hetton-le-Hole on a Saturday afternoon to the 'penny rush' that showed a number of trailer films made for plenty of shouting. On their way home a detour was made to the old pit heaps which were just right for squatting down and sliding with their boots down the sides of the heaps and getting a telling-off from mother for coming home all dusty and dirty.

When the Salvation Army had 'lantern evenings', it was a jam jar entrance. At Sunday afternoon chapel meetings [you] used to get a star on your card for attendance. These were good because when the time came for them to give a trip to the seaside these stars were useful because if you had a certain amount it was free.

G.A.

You were somebody if you sat there

Saturday morning's friend, Eileen, and myself used to go to the Saturday Morning Club at the Palace Picture House. We tried to join the Havelock Picture House but it was full. Now this club was for children. We used to watch a cartoon, a serial (the one I remembered was *Smiling Jack*) and the big picture. Between the serial and the picture some children would do a turn, singing, dancing or even whistling. You had to audition the night before. Two ladies were in charge – one on the piano, the other one introducing. We called them Auntie Gray and Auntie Edith. Eileen and myself used to go on the stage and dance. My mam made us our costumes from rolls of cotton wool and old pink sheets. Then the next Saturday we could sit in the circle seats. You were somebody if you sat there.

M.H.

For years I worked in the tattie fields

I was born at No. 4 Bell Street, Millfield, in the year 1912, but at six month we shifted down to No. 23 Sans Street down in Hendon. We moved into an old doctor's house, whose name escapes me. But I know it was also next to a blacksmith's shop, by the name of Campbell, who shod all the horses' hooves for all the horses that trod the streets of Hendon. Many a time we would be awoken when the horses banged their hooves against the bedroom walls. For years I worked in the tattie fields to help out the bit income that we had, and I have seen the time when I worked in a fish shop, chopping and preparing the chips just to get a free fish lot as wages. That was at Barratt's fish shop, in Sans Street. I had seven brothers and five sisters.

J.P.

We got tuppence a week pocket money

We got tuppence a week pocket money on a Saturday in 1930. The Roker Cinema, near the Fort pub… cost tuppence for posh seats in the circle but only a penny downstairs. You could then have a ha'p'ny for sweets and a ha'p'ny ride home on the tram… One silent film showed Mary Pickford and her man struggling across a swamp with a crying baby. She cut a finger off her glove, put a tiny hole in the end and fixed it on a medicine bottle to feed this baby. I never asked where the milk came from, how she made the hole, nor how she kept the finger on the bottle, or even where the bottle came from. We were just in a magic world where we accepted what happened and went home, (walking or riding), happy.

P.S.

Dad, mam's had twins

I remember a very special day in July 1945. We lived in St Mark's Road North, in Millfield and dad worked at the National Galvanisers, which was opposite Doxford's shipyard. At twelve noon, all the men rushed out of work to make their way home for dinner. They came up Millfield back lane, along Aiskell Street where they crossed over Hylton Road, then on to St Mark's Road.

On this day, I arrived home from school to find that the stork had brought me twin brothers. Imagine my excitement… I was only ten years of age. I heard the buzzer… I wanted to be first to give my dad the good news. I ran into the street and was confronted with a sea of faces. I ran through the crowd of men shouting, 'dad, mam's had twins!' When I eventually reached him, he gave me a big hug. I think that he must have been in shock. He smiled when the men simultaneously raised their caps and cheered. This was a sight that I will never forget.

L.C.

I never knew my father very much

I was born on 3 June 1926 at No. 4 Pemberton Street, Hendon: a typical tenement house. We lived downstairs and there were two more families lived upstairs. My family was grandfather, mam and dad, three sisters, two brothers and me – a big family, but that was quite common those days. I never knew my father very much when I was little, because he went to sea – sailed all over the world. When he came home he went to the pubs with his mates until the money ran out, then back to sea. I remember one day I was sitting on the stairs with Alan Murray who lived upstairs – we were about five years old – a woman came out of our house and gave us some cream cakes and a sandwich to eat. We didn't know why but we thought it was great. A little later on in life I learned that was the day of my grandfather's funeral.

T.B.

We were taught to have good manners

Now on a Sunday morning while my mother cooked the dinner we had to go to church on Sunday morning and Sunday School in the afternoon (All Saints) and church at night. As our mother and father were good Christian people, we were taught to have good manners.

We always said our grace and thanked God for our blessings. We were also taught to respect our elders. I remember quite plain going to our aunt's house and as soon as we went in she would say, 'will you have a piece of cake?' and we would say, 'no, thank-you'. She would say, 'ho yes I know, your mother has told you always to say no thank you and don't be greedy', then my aunt would give us some cake and we would say 'thank you very much'.

E.M.

Ear wax and black horse-hair

From the age of five until seven I seemed to spend lots of time with grown-ups. My mother was a qualified piano teacher and, as she taught schoolchildren, it was mostly after tea they had their lessons, so I had to sit in the kitchen or go to my grandmother's. Grandmother had four spinster sisters who made a fuss of me, took me visiting their friends. I also had to recite or sing to them. I remember one lady had an ear trum-pet. I hated having to recite into this contrap-tion because it smelt of ear wax, very strongly. Another friend who lived in South Shields had this black horse-hair sofa, it was awful for a little girl with bare legs to sit on and not shuffle about, so that's why this must stick in my memory.

D.L.

That was our New Year

Oh well, New Year was a special day in our lives because it was always spent at our grand-mother's house. All the children would go to bed on an afternoon so we could all stay up. All the clippie mats were put in the yard and all the furniture, so there was plenty of room for all when the family came. There was no drink allowed, only ginger wine, but we always had a good time – we used to sing and dance all night right though till the next day. At teatime her own sisters came from Newcastle to join in the festivity and that was our New Year.

M.P.

Orphanage boys, c. 1910. They received a high standard of education, three good meals a day and were well clothed.

Remained there until they died

In the grounds of the Municipal General Hospital were the Cottage Homes. In here poor, abandoned and neglected children were accommodated. I was a medical secretary and used to accompany the medical superintendent when each new batch of children arrived to be examined, to see if they were well enough to stay in the home. Some of these children were given daily jobs around the hospital. Some were strange but lovable little folk. I say little for I recall Andy and Pele. I think they were just 4ft plus. They were paid a shilling a week. They remained there until they died.

M.F.

During the snows of 1947

During the snows of 1947 we all got sent home from school, so we rolled a snowball until it was so big we dug out the inside and made an igloo and next day my mam took me and friends to Mowbray Park. The pond was

Mary Simms, the maypole princess, Old Orphanage, late 1940s.

Sunderland orphanage children.

frozen, but not as much as I thought, so when I walked on it I fell through just near the edge. Still, my wellies filled up with icy water and I didn't feel so good when I got home off the bus with frozen feet.

M.A.

I wanted a goldfish

I remember when I was quite young. I wanted a goldfish and someone told me that the rag man, who came around the street with his horse and cart, gave you a goldfish in return for rags. Next time I heard the rag man calling out I gave him my dad's best trousers. I was thrilled. I got my fish and a balloon. Sadly, my excitement and pleasure soon disappeared when my dad found out what I had done. All hell broke loose in our house that day!

O.H.

How we loved our penny rides

During the late 1940s, in Hendon, there was a man who used to come around the street with his pony and trap, calling out, 'a penny a ride!'. The pony was so gentle and the trap was gaily painted with bright colours. For a penny we were taken down the street and up the next street, back to where we started from. The trap held about eight children and oh! How we loved our penny rides. Then there was the 'rag man': he came around the back lanes and for a bundle of rags we were given a baby chicken or a goldfish. We also had singers that came round the streets, they stood in the middle of the road and sang. People would go out and give them a copper, whatever they could afford. Some of these men had beautiful voices. Then there was the fish barrows, pushed round the streets, laden with fish and willicks (whelks). His call was 'calla herring'. A big bag of willicks was 3d.

A.H.

The Mecca of dancing

As a boy in the 1920s I spent hours playing on and around the bandstand… The robust structure withstood the treatment it received from us children climbing about and swinging on the metalwork – a forerunner for the modern children's climbing frame. The iron work was painted brown or black. It was situated at the edge of the moor. The bandstand had no roof or cover, completely open to the elements. An area of ground approximately twenty-five yards square, covered by concrete, smooth surface – this was the dance floor. The Mecca of dancing for Eastenders… The area was known as the 'Flat'. Many a pair of shoes were worn out due to the waltz, foxtrot, Boston two step. The bandstand itself was positioned at the south-east end of the 'Flat'. The bandstand was frequently used – once a week on a Wednesday evening, during the summer months. Seats were a fixture – planks of wood embedded in the ground.

A.H.

It was a fantastic treat to us

Once in a while we had a special treat, a trip from home in South Hylton into Sunderland. A bus ride to Hylton Road School, then a tram ride to central station, a short walk down Union Street and into Jacky White's Market. They sold everything imaginable. First stop for us was the stall that sold American comics, then on to a fruiterer's for a bag of blood oranges and a bag of monkey nuts with shells on for dad. Liquorice Allsorts from the next stall and maybe a rabbit for Sunday's dinner. Then a sit in the huge brass scales to see how heavy we were. Next was a visit to the Betta Pie shop for some of their juicy steak pies to take home for dinner. Then it was back home, feeling well satisfied with our trip out. Not a lot by today's standards, but it was a fantastic treat to us, especially as our dad was on the dole.

B.G.

My father used to take me across the ferry

I was born in Hedworth Street. I often reminisce about the 'old days', and that area of Monkwearmouth riverside known throughout my lifetime, and before, as 'the Barbary Coast'... For transport we used the 'Hap'ny Ferry' to the East End. At the bottom of High Street East there was the 'Old Market'. My father used to take me across the ferry. The sweets were all a penny a quarter. He would buy me a coloured balloon. When we returned everyone's lovely balloons floated above the ferry passengers.

E.G.

A great adventure for me

It was as a guide that I was able to have my first 'grown-up' holiday. We often went on hikes in the country near Sunderland, taking the bus for a short distance to get out of town and then spending the rest of the day walking in lanes or along the riverbank. In the early months of 1943 our guider suggested that we might like to go youth hostelling, walking in Northumberland and sleeping at night in a different hostel each night. We went by bus to Hexham, a market town about thirty miles from home, and from there followed a circular route, walking between ten and fifteen miles each day and returning to Hexham after five days. Not very exciting by the standards of today, but a great adventure for me.

A.M.

I attended clarinet lessons

Miss Gertrude Anderson and her sister were two Victorian women who lived in Winifred Street near Mowbray Park where even the piano legs were modestly shrouded in leggings. Miss Anderson's first professional engagement was at the Sunderland Empire as violinist in the orchestra. She rented two attic rooms in Lourdes House, an Edwardian property where she had a music and practice room. Here the decor was also Victorian, with lots

St Peter's Cubs 1931, in St Peter's Hall.

of lace cloths and antimacassars. Eventually St Anthony's Roman Catholic Girls' Grammar School took over the building. From 1957 I attended clarinet lessons with Miss Anderson. I was proud to be part of Sunderland Youth Orchestra and rehearsed in Cowan Street School, later in Southmoor School.

M.M.

The only country we ever saw

We lived in Monkwearmouth near J.L. Thompson's shipyard surrounded by small narrow streets with chimneys that belched out smoke all day long, summer and winter, with back lanes, corner shops, pubs, shipyards and factories. The only countryside we ever saw was when dad walked my sister and I down the Dene (now Dene Estate) where he had an allotment. We would spend a bit of time pottering about playing about before leaving, picking a bunch of flowers for mam. Dad always put on a lovely show and grew lots of vegetables in a garden to be proud of.

He would take our hands and walk us by the cemetery wall, which led onto a small wooden bridge; a stream flowed underneath with watercress growing by the edge. We would skip along a narrow country lane with Holmes Farm in the distance with cattle grazing. Before returning home we would gather the watercress to go with the lettuce and tomatoes we had picked for tea. Mam would be waiting with a can of Spam and a small loaf of bread cut and thinly spread with 'marg' (no butter). We did this every week.

J.Q.

The sights we never saw 'cause we fell asleep

The Festival of Britain was meant to give everyone a lift in 1951 and 250 girls from Bede Girls' Grammar School went on a visit to our capital city. It cost £2.10 (which was half a week's wage) so we paid weekly. We met at 11 p.m. on Thursday night, at the south end of the station. Miss Norman got no sleep as we sat

Corporation Quay area from J.L. Thompson's, 1973.

Barnes Park, pre-1914.

all night just talking and laughing. The exhibition was scientifically based. Most memorable were the Skylon and the early television – tiny black and white in the Dome of Discovery. Escalators were amazing, to go on the tube train to the corner house café for tea. We went on a bus trip to see London, we thought it was dark and sooty. The sights we never saw 'cause we all fell asleep. We returned overnight and had to go to school in the morning.

J.Q.

Everyone had bad teeth

In 1933 I started school. Like many five-year-olds, I had to get teeth out. Nobody seemed to have toothbrushes, but everyone had bad teeth. Mam took me to the education office in John Street: the dentist had his surgery there. I had to use the toilet in their backyard, then sit up in a chair and get gas. Lots of other five-year-olds, and their mothers were milling about. After I came round I was given a white pad to hold over my mouth. Everyone got a white pad. Everyone spit blood. John Street pavements were all spits of blood. People looked at me, with my pad over my mouth; I felt quite brave. Mam took me home and it was good having her all to myself with no little ones to spoil the day.

J.R.

One day a friend pushed me into the duck pond

As a youngster I spent many happy days in Barnes Park with my mam and friends. We climbed onto the cannon, listened to the bands and, of course, fed the ducks. Unfortunately one day a 'friend' pushed me into the slimy end of the duck pond. Soaking wet and quite smelly I was marched home to Ormond Street by my mam. On reaching home my dad saw the funny side of the situation, and we all ended up laughing.

N.S.

In the snowy winters it was splendid for tobogganing

When I was young in the early 1920s, my home in the Craiglands at the bottom of Strawberry Bank, was opposite Strawberry Cottage which had surrounding fields of vegetables and a herd of dairy cows from which came our daily pintas, delivered in galvanised cans with tightly fitting cup-shaped lids. Nearby were a few old pear trees, their fruit small and uninviting, but delicious when ripe. In snowy winters the bank was splendid for tobogganing. Halfway up the bank was a small freshwater stream much loved by our visiting dog.

J.S.

The Victoria Hall and Mowbray park Sunderland, pre-1914.

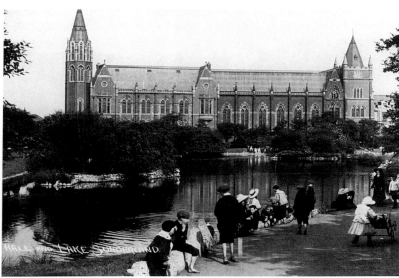

The Victoria Hall and Mowbray park, Sunderland, pre-1914.

I was a guest of honour at the ceremony

My uncle was killed in the crush of the Victoria Hall disaster in 1883. Hundreds of children rushed down the stairs to get to the stage for free sweets and the door at the bottom couldn't be opened inwards for the crush of bodies. Afterwards a law was passed that all exit doors in public buildings must open outwards. A memorial sculpture in white showed a mother holding a limp child across her arms all enclosed in a… high, domed glass case. When it was moved from Bishopwearmouth to Mowbray Park I was a guest of honour at the ceremony.

C.S.

two

Home and
Lifestyle

From left to right: Oswald Brantingham, (1906-76); George Brantingham, (1911-92) and Elsie Brantingham, (1902-82).

Bath night in front of a lovely fire

Another lovely time we looked forward to was the Roker Jazz Band. On Saturday nights we would get out the old zinc bath – bath night in front of a lovely fire. Then wait for the band coming back. Most times with the winning cup. It was so exciting.

E.G.

We had gas lighting

We had gas lighting when I was a child and you could depend on it that when I was asked to light the gas mantle, I would put the lighted paper through it, no matter how hard I tried to do it carefully – it was such a fine filament it broke easily. You would put a penny in the gas meter, then the gas man used to come around and empty the meter every so often; he would pile the pennies up in rows of twelve then maybe we would get five shillings back. We as children would get a copper out of it. We were quids in when the gas man came.

W.D.

Our backyard

My job on a Friday evening or a Saturday morning was to swill the red bricks with a stiff 'yard broom'. If mam decided it wasn't clean I had to do it all again. Our backyard had a dog kennel, a rabbit hutch, a rain-water barrel… and a standpipe to supply all domestic water needs. At the bottom of the yard we had a flush toilet and a coal house. We had a 'garden' in two motor-car tyres, a clothes line and space to park our bikes. We had a half glass shed with an enamel dish for washing and, of course, a galvanised bath hanging on the backyard wall… If you lost your ball over someone else's wall you had to go and ask for it back politely.

T.B.

My nana

My nana lived in a pit cottage in Bond Street, with a fire burning coal which granda' got free to heat his bath water etc. I saw flies whacked with a rolled-up newspaper or trapped on a strip of sticky paper hanging from the ceiling. Mice were bad and cockroaches used to scatter about on the lino when it was dark and quiet. Nana used to wear long-legged pink bloomers and whale-bone stays made by Spirella. A woman came to the house and measured nana, then payments were collected week by week.

S.F.

Me dad rented a telly

I was eighteen when Princess Elizabeth was crowned Queen in Westminster Abbey.

East-End family life, a typical backyard photograph.

Our field was always covered in coal dust

The small pit cottage in Sunderland where I was born was called Colliery Square. It had brown painted stairs, with no carpet on, where we played. We lived in a row of cottages with a field in front, then Monkwearmouth coal pit. Our field was always covered in coal dust from the pit, but in winter when it snowed the field became a magic place, when I would spend hours looking out of the window when the snow twinkled like stars at night, with the glow from the street lights above Monkwearmouth colliery.

M.O.

When I was a child living in the East End

When I was a child living in the East End in the 1930s, High Street was a very busy street, with Liverpool House department store dominating the scene, and the store had the overhead pay-box rails, which I loved to watch whizzing along the ceiling. There was the Salvation Army hostel, where we, the children of the area, would peer in and see the men 'derelicts' getting a pot of cocoa and doorstop bread for the night, also see the cubicles they slept in – these smelt a bit. There was the old market, which started at the top of James Williamson Street and went down to High Street... There were three pork shops, post office, doctor's and chemist's; it was like a contained place, all on its own. My mother never went up to the town, as she called it. As children we were sent to buy pieces of bacon at Harrison's and stale cakes from Binns in Fawcett Street, also bruised fruit from Whittaker's. We would come back with a lot of food for a few coppers, as we were only sent for cast-offs. The transport at this time was horse and carts and if the men wanted to move things they hired handcarts: we had one when we went to the beach for coal.

W.D.

We must have been the only ones round our doors, judging by the number of people who came to our house, when me dad rented a telly from Rediffusion. It was 3ft high, standing on the floor, a rich mahogany veneered walnut-colour wood with two doors opening to reveal a titchy television screen on top, with a black and white screen. I helped me mam to make tea and sandwiches and we had a bit of a sing-song after the ceremony finished. When the choir chanted 'Elizabeth Regina', goosebumps came on my arms. The coronation was shown at the pictures after, but the sharing round the telly was the best experience.

M.H.

Beach scene, Hendon, c. 1900.

of them just lived in one room – I can name quite a few of them – and most of them have done very well for themselves... it's wonderful to see how people have made the most of things. I wouldn't say it was a poor upbringing in Monkwearmouth, because there was always food on the table for the children.

J.C.

There were a lot of characters around...

There was a whole family lived on Cage Hill – the Maskells – they were all ginger and they lived in this little cottage. One of them, a grandson, turned out to be a priest so it just goes to show how people have improved themselves. There were a lot of characters around – there was Catty Allen, she was a character, and she had the rag shop. There was Tommy the cobbler, he was so bow-legged, but he could mend a pair of shoes in half an hour. There were the Mackenzies; they were big names at St Peter's. There was Valente's ice-cream shop, Jack Smith's. You couldn't imagine how many people lived there.

J.C.

Ten a penny

Most traders sold their products from hand-carts or horse and cart. You could hear the milkman shouting, 'milko'. Ma would send me out for a 'gill' of milk if she couldn't afford a pint. We got it from the huge churn on the back of the cart. The fishwoman pushed her barrow round shouting, 'ten a penny, calla her-ring'. A young woman from the East End sold brandy snaps, 'ha'p'ny a bag'.

E.G.

There was always food on the table

It was known as the Barbary Coast; there were about four tenants in one building, most

No shawls allowed...

You were talking about the women, not being allowed in Binns Store with shawls on... It is possible that they watched anybody coming in with a shawl on very closely, or even with a cape, which old women still wore when I was a kid. Because I suppose they could have put things underneath quite easily. But I'd rather fancy if anyone went into Binns with just a shawl over their head, some of them went about in those days, they would very soon get out, because they would get short shrift so to speak, they wouldn't be wanted there. I don't know if they'd actually be asked to leave. But I think they would be made to feel thoroughly

David Goldman's shop, Rutland Street, Pallion, Sunderland, 1970.

Billy Baker's butcher's shop, Hendon Road, Sunderland, Christmas 1921.

Brumwell's, High Street, West Sunderland.

uncomfortable because they would sort of be followed around. There were a lot of floor-walkers employed in those days…

M.H.

That was the way it was

I often reminisce about the old days and that area of Monkwearmouth riverside known… as 'the Barbary Coast'. Hedworth Street and others were mainly tenements… Often four families to a house, a large family of six children meant eight people sharing the one bedroom. Today it sounds terrible, but that was the way – it was the way of life.

E.G.

There seemed a lot of Italian families

In and around Sans Street there seemed a lot of Italian families. There was Peter and Nellie Minchella with their sons Johnny and Tony; Joe Geraldi; Frankie Pucci; Joe Baldersara; Joe Valente and, of course, Peter Someo, that lived in nearby New Gray Street. One of the Italian families had an ice-cream parlour that was situated in Sans Street, and his name was Frankie Pucci. We would always be in his ice-cream parlour drinking his small glasses of Vantas, which tasted very nice, in fact it tasted just like Coca Cola is today. All of these Italians made their ice cream in their own houses, then went around the streets of Hendon to sell their… halfpenny ice-cream cornets, in their handcarts and they all seemed to make a good living out of it.

J.P.

We had various characters visit the street

We had various characters visit the street, which we looked forward to. There was the knife grinder on his bike – we loved giving him knives to grind, and we watched in

The Half Moon Inn, High Street East, Sunderland, 1930s.

The old East End Market, Sunderland.

Burleigh Street, Sunderland, 6 May 1935.

fascination as he sharpened them. A fish merchant used to sell fish from the back of his van, (what would health and safety think of that now?). He used to announce his arrival in the street shouting, 'caller herring, caller herring' to bring the housewives out. The candy man would come with his horse and cart, shouting, 'any lumber?' and we would pester our mothers to part with something to claim our balloons. The fruit and veg' man who came around, he had lost an arm in the First World War and fascinated us children when he used to draw potatoes etc to the front of the cart by using his hook. A cheer would go up every evening when the lamplighter appeared with his long stick, to light the gas lamps. He too was a disabled ex-serviceman from the First World War.

M.R.

People in Monkwearmouth were the salt of the earth

In the 1940s and '50s people in Monkwearmouth were the salt of the earth; the community spirit was great. You could leave your house doors wide open day or night and nobody would dream of entering unless invited. My mother would leave the milk, rent and tallyman monies on the hall table in full view of every-

The wedding of George Kirkup Brantingham, (1890-1961) and Gertrude Brantingham (neé Spencer), (1888-1975).

one: it would never be touched. Neighbours would all muck in, especially at a birth, when the local elder women would act as midwives and also feed the husband. His mates would then take the irate father to the local cooper. If it was a long birth then it was a good excuse for a lock-in – talk about wetting the baby's head: there were times when you could have drowned the poor little thing! Also if there was illness, accidents or other misfortunes, the spirit was there. For example, a young girl went missing one day, she did not come home at the time she was supposed to, the whole street turned out until they found her. She'd fallen down a gully and broken her leg.

C.W.

Corner of Anne Street,
Deptford, Sunderland.

Fosters shop, No. 18 Ogle
Terrace, Low Southwick.

The Palatine Hotel,
Sunderland.

The most shops I can recollect in Monkwearmouth

The most shops I can recollect in Monkwearmouth – there were many – were ones on the corner of Victor Street, middle block where ah lived with me mam and dad. On our side was White's fruit and vegetables, run by Norman and his wife Mary. There was always a barra standin' outside the shop. He was norra young man but Norman would pull the barra hesell down the back lanes sellin' his stock. His goods were cheap and best quality.

On the opposite corner was Meggie Lowton's sweet and grocery shop, which was all dilapidated and one side boarded up. Meggie was always smartly dressed, never without a hat and in winter time she wore a real fur coat, even when servin'. She cut the meat with a grit big carvin' knife. Her nails were manicured. She kept an enamel bowl o' water on the side and she washed her hands everytime she cut the meat. The best she sold was chopped pork. You could smell it as she sliced it, better than boiled ham. Startin' at the top of the bottom block was Gannie Mitchie's. She must have been eighty if she was a day. You could buy anythin' and everythin' off her, from candles to flour: the place was crowded with stuff. Best of all for us young ones was her sticky golden toffee cakes.

All gone now but the memories of those happy childhood days and the corner shops will stay with me till the end of my days.

J.D.

Monday was always clothes-washing day

I was born 1922 and as a child Monday was always clothes-washing day. My mother and her sister, my auntie Mary, would be up at 5 a.m. to stoke the old boiler fire, to heat the water. They took their turn, one carrying the water and one carrying the empty pail, to fill the poss-tub up which was already set up in the backyard with two poss sticks. They threw the clothes in and would poss the clothes, one up and one down. After that they would wring all the clothes out by hand. The ash-pit men used to come around the streets at the same time and if it was a really windy day by the time they opened the old wooden middens, as we call them, the old man used to put his shovel in and as he fetched it out the wind would blow the ash and the papers, toilet paper today, all over the street. As the washing would be drying on lines in the street the women would be furious, as the paper would stick to the washing.

And then of course Tuesday would be ironing. Yes, Monday would be washing day, I would think, in our house, and then of course Tuesday would be ironing, the ironing had to be done, and then there were many bigger families, and such a lot of washing to be done that it was a two day job and even probably the next day would be baking day, which fell each week.

Friday was the day for the fire irons, that was what we called the weekend cleaning. If anyone had brickyards, pen brickyards, the pails of soapy water or anything like that was poured onto the yard, and the men, a lot of the men used to scrub the yards with the broom.

Mr R.

Once I got my fingers trapped in the mangle

We had a coal fire to heat the oven where my mam cooked especially lovely bread. We heated flat irons on the fire and I was allowed to iron hankies and pillowcases when I was eight, but she did shirts and things. We cleaned the hot iron by rubbing it in a tray of sand and spit on it to check the heat. The spit jumped off if it was hot enough. She cleaned the brass fireside surround every Friday. Washing was hung out to dry in the yard or all over the living room if it was rainy, which was horrible. Once I got my fingers trapped in the mangle and still have the scar after seventy years. We had a line of bowls to rinse once, then again, then the dolly blue to make the white things look whiter.

A.B.

The making of clippie mats

And the brasses, why me mother used to take the brass rod down off the mantle shelf and get the Meppo tin out and I used to be sitting sometimes reading a comic or watching her and she used to be up and down the pole, rubbing it, and you could really see your face in the gear that was on the fireplace: at the time, like the kettle, it had to be kept clean and also the old fire irons. And in regard to the house itself, the hobbies in them days, as one of the pastimes was the old clippie mats, which I have done myself, many a time, my mother used to cut up the old rags, (coats, caps anything with bonny colours in), into two-inch-long strips and she used to go to the Co-operative store and buy yarn and put it onto the mat frames and I've sat many an hour with me mother, knitting, and just following the pattern; and then the great moment arrived when we used to unfold it out, unfurl it out on the floor and then me mother used to get down on her hands and knees and go over the top, cutting the extra long pieces off with her scissors and they were really happy times…

Mr R.

We put her in a shoe box

I bathed Terry and got him ready for bed. 7 p.m. or later I had twinges of pain, it felt like labour… I was seven-month pregnant. The midwife Sister Burns thought I couldn't be in labour but when she examined me she screamed, 'you're in labour'. It was now twenty to twelve, baby on its way and breach. My sister Kitty ran home as the screams were unearthly (no gas and air); baby was born with umbilical cord around her neck twice and once around her body. The baby was in distress. The midwife put her on a small scale weighing in at 2lb 4oz. Sister Burns says, 'oh I won't get paid for my taxi fair to get home before midnight.' So I suggested putting the baby down as born on the 14 February at twenty past twelve. We put her in a shoe box and packed her with cotton wool. Florrie watched over her all night. The hospital wing was just getting built for premature babies. The doctor came the next day with a premature bag, cotton wool and hot-water bottles. I had to wake her every two hours for a feed. They didn't think she would survive the day. She's now fifty-three, Elizabeth Carol Bell McGuinness.

B.B.

A tonsils operation on the kitchen table

Before NHS my mother paid weekly into Dr Blakey's club. It can't have been much and it meant she did not have to face a large bill to visit or call him out. He had a practice in Fordfield Place. My friend Mary's brother had a tonsils operation on the kitchen table; her mother had to give it a good scrub down first. Doctors always walked straight into a house as the front door was always open. Once we found a doctor due to call next door in our backyard. He had walked along the passage straight from the wrong front door into the back!

E.H.

The appointments system

In the 1950s we had a family Dr K., who was a right character. It didn't pay to be of a shy nature as his voice was so loud all the patients in the waiting room knew all about your ailments by the time you emerged. The appointments system was: arrive as early as you can and sit in a row on what looked like a tram seat, curved, with wooden slats. Latecomers just formed a queue, sometimes out the door! Doctor would enter on a Monday morning, pause at his door and boom, 'If any of you are bad with the beer you can go home now!' Yet we knew him as a man who visited, making sure you were treated for whooping cough and measles, chicken pox and tonsillitis. He advised your mam on tonics if you were 'rundown'. He sterilised his ear instruments in the coal fire to relieve yet another earache. Not always liked because of his straight talking, he had much to value.

R.P.

You can examine me through my clothes

We had to live with my auntie Nellie who we called Mama Dahl in the Waterman's tavern in Turnbull Street. We were sheltered from the worst poverty. When we asked to go in our bare feet like the other children at St John's School she said, 'You can go in your bare feet with your shoes on'. She did not drink alcohol as she saw what it did to people but, 'for medicinal purposes only', she would sometimes sip brandy and hot water and sugar... Mama Dahl was a terrible prude. She would say to the doctor 'you can examine me through my clothes' when he needed to listen to her chest.

M.S.

Me mother scalded both arms

Me mother scalded both arms trying to save toffee she was making falling on the floor. That's the first time I learned how to bake a stone of bread. I was twelve years old and I baked then. She used to bake a stone of bread every other day and a half a stone of teacakes... There was ten of us.

S.N.

To me it was the workhouse

In 1937 I definitely did not want my wife to go to the maternity hospital to have our first baby, because to me it was the workhouse. Only the lowest people went there, but she insisted because her mother had died of puerperal fever after the home birth of her fourth baby

The Waterman's tavern, Sunderland.

The Donnison School and the old Sunderland workhouse on Church Walk.

in Barrack Street in the East End. In those days women in the area acted as midwives and hygiene was not an issue.

J.P.

Extractions. Have you ever been gassed?

I only got a small bag of sweets on a Saturday that was my ration in the war so I used to cut up the dolly mixtures into four tiny bits before I went on the bus, with my 6d for the pictures across the water. I can't remember cleaning my teeth when I was little, so eventually I had to go for fillings and extractions at the school dentists in Southwick and Smyrna Place. What butchers they all were! Drilling without painkillers. Harsh words if you dared to cry. Extractions? Have you ever been gassed? An awful smell as the mask was plonked on your face, slipping into darkness and spinning round and round in ever-decreasing circles until you woke up just as you were being sucked into the big swirling black hole in the middle. Terrifying. Horrible.

S.P.

When the women were confined

In the street where I lived as a child all babies were born at the home, delivered by a midwife. When the women were confined, as they used to describe it, women in the street would help look after other children in the family. Cook meals and get the children ready for bed etc, it was a street event. The lady next door had twins. What excitement! It was a tradition at christenings always that the family gave a piece of cheese to the first child they met of the opposite sex of the baby for the good luck to be shared. In the baby's first outing a piece of silver (usually a sixpence in those days) would be placed in the pram by neighbours to bring baby luck. Similarly the first time a new mother visited a house with her baby, gifts of

sugar, bread and a piece of coal were given to ensure the child would have sweetness, substance and always have a fire throughout life. These traditions seem now to have died out.

M.R.

Lice were removed with a fine-tooth comb

At school loads of kids had gentian violet painted on their faces and limbs for impetigo. Some had ringworm. Others got sent to Southwick clinic or Smyrna Place and had their heads shaved because of head lice. One or two caught and died from diphtheria. People got jars of Virol, a sweet brown viscous iron tonic and had sun-ray treatment for vitamin D. Whooping cough was common and a few went to Grindon Sanatorium for fresh air and rest to recover from tuberculosis. I got boils which my mother treated. Lice were removed with a fine-tooth comb, very painful on my hair. Me mam curled with rags into ringlets every night. The captured lice she squashed on the comb with her thumb nail then threw them on the open coal fire.

S.P.

There were lots of children running about in bare feet

There were lots of children running about in bare feet, especially paper boys, but there was an organisation, called the Hudson's Fund, and seemly teachers at school used to put children forward for this fund and they used to get free shoes; they would go to Mitchell's in High Street for them. You wonder how people existed but they always managed; the oven was always on, you could go for a penn' worth of pot stuff, you got a turnip, a leak, and an onion, and soup was a main thing, there was bacon bones and neck ends and things like that to make soup.

J.C.

Sunderland's East End, c. 1901.

Ma, the bairn wants the titty…

People were all very friendly and the older children used to bring the babies in, all wrapped up, and I don't know whether I should say this but they used to be wrapped in a shawl, there was a big grating and they would shout, 'ma the bairn wants the titty'. The mother would come out and sit on a little form just inside, feed the baby, wrap it up and send it back home again. As I said all the women were very friendly but there again there was a saying, 'you'll be the talk of the big washhouse'. But saying that they were all lovely people, never ever owed my mother anything as I say she had the tick slate and on top of that she used to say 'as long as I get the money to pay in', sometimes they owed as much as one and six.

J.C.

Obviously I did not know what a 'parish' was

In the 1930s my father was a plasterer. He always had work in the summer but during the winter his employers wouldn't employ him because of the frost; we were always badly off in the winter. One day, slightly before I started school, I heard the first words about the 'parish'; obviously I did not know what a 'parish' was and it was being held in the Cloisters, Stockton Road. My mother put her black shawl on and I went up with her; they took her into a room and when she came out she was crying, they had turned her down for the parish fund, as I had nine brothers and sisters: she was worried. My father would try and make money in the winter by chopping sticks and going to the beach to pick coal. There were lots of people in the same boat

Cycling was a very popular recreation from the late nineteenth century onwards.

and they would try and help each other out; my maternal grandmother was always very good. When things were particularly bad, she would take one or two of us to live with her... There was a Pearson's Fresh Air Fund – you were given vouchers for shoes, groceries and clothes. You took the shoe vouchers to Michelle's, High Street. We all wore soft shoes; at this time they were like modern gym shoes. The clothes vouchers were taken to Liverpool House, High Street.

W.D.

There was no redundancy money

There was parish relief in those days. If you had a piano and a sideboard you got nothing at all. When the parish man came they used to get the neighbours to carry the piano out and hide it in their houses and lock them 'cause the children played the pianos and if the parish man heard you, you would get prison.

S.N.

Some wore socks with their toes poking out

In the 1930s Sunderland was divided into the East End and the West End. Children in the Crowtree Road area wore plimsolls. Some wore socks with their toes poking out. There were ladies in black skirts and shawls, hard working to make a few coppers. An exciting thing for me to do on a Saturday was to have a lovely shining sixpence to spend in Woolworths, selling ice cream, sweets, toys, and comics.

E.H.

What would they pawn?

Anything they could lay their hands on: bedding, clothing, taking just pinafores, anything like that, only got tuppence and three pence for them. One thing that we found, which rather amazed us, was the old cut-throat razor. A woman said she pawned it because he threatened to cut her throat with it, and she'd put it out of his road, got about nine pence for it. There was a man called Sammy Berger, that had a pawn shop down this way and it was a regular thing for them to talk about going to Sammy's... he was a Jew. But sometimes you know what that money was for? To either drink or to put on a horse; sometimes it would be a necessity, they'd want it for food, granted, but it went on other things as well.

M.H.

It's keeping poor people poor

There was another thing that went on which used to horrify us when we heard it was happening. You know there was a club woman

Vaux Maxim ale truck, 'a highly nourishing stout'.

who let them leave orders to go to the shops and you got the goods and of course you paid. If you got one for a pound you paid twenty-one shillings back. The woman in turn got her half-crown to the pound off the shop, that was her livelihood. If she didn't get paid by the customer, well that was just too bad, because she was the loser. But what used to happen, they used to go out and get an order like that from the club woman and supposing they got it for a pound, they would go and find somebody who was fairly affluent and they would sell it for fourteen shillings for the thing and they had twenty-one shillings to pay back. I've seen my cousin nearly in tears over this, because she used to say, 'It's keeping poor people poor and they shouldn't do it, they're never going to get out of debt.'

M.H.

I was sent to the Dole School

When I got finished at the laundry, I was sent to the Dole School, this was at the Wheatsheaf; it was what you called the Colliery School years ago. This is what happened if you were not working. Under sixteen went on a morn-ing, and over sixteen to eighteen went on an afternoon. We used to get a bottle of milk and two chocolate biscuits for our break. We used to get our dole to keep us off the streets.

P.W.

I was one of the lucky ones

I never went on any holiday but I tell you what I did... We were poor, me dad didn't have much work and there used to be a fund for poor children – I don't know if you know – it was called the Priestman Fund. Now I was one of the lucky ones who used to gain from this fund. Every six months you were taken to a shop, in fact it was Jopling's in the town. I used to go and be rigged out from top to bottom out of this fund. That was a big day in my life to get them new clothes. I mean, you know me mam, she used to pull my sister's clothes down for me, but I never used to mind getting cast-offs. We never went hungry, I mean you know mam used to cook and always made bread teacakes and things. I don't think money is that important to anybody as long as you have enough to pay your way.

M.P.

Fawcett Street, Sunderland, 1953.

Hylton Road, Sunderland.

We went down to the beach for coal

When I was a child and before I went to school, my mother would borrow an old pram and we went down to the beach for coal. I was shown what to look for. When the coal was placed on the fire it would spit and I was on watch and would have to shout if a piece of coal jumped out onto the carpet, which made small burn–holes.

M.W.

We baked everything at home…

Oh, my mother was a marvellous cook and we did everything of course, they were coun-try people to start with, who had been used always to having a big garden and everything to hand. And… she still did the whole, you know jamming and pickling and all that kind of thing was done in the home and certainly baking. Alison's – we still have an Alison's Mill – they used to have a shop in Hendon Road, where we used to get our flour. There was three stone of flour and a quarter of a stone of wholemeal every week and that was baked up. And one day when Kitty had gone with the order, the woman that was in the shop said, 'you must have a good sale for bread'. She said, 'well what do you mean? We don't sell bread'. She said, 'well what on earth do you do with

Above: *Mackies' Corner Sunderland.*

Right: *Hylton Road above Millfield Station, 1925 or 1926, outside the Mountain Daisy.*

it?', 'Well eat it of course.' And when she came home she was most indignant: 'mother, that woman in Alison's thinks we own a shop and sell bread because we get a lot of flour.' But, you know, teacakes, pies and everything we baked at home.

M.H.

There was only one tripe shop

In Sans Street there was a nice pie shop that was very popular. It was called Hughie Lynch's Pie Shop and he only had one arm. But he still managed to bake his nice pies. The biggest drawback in Sans Street was that there was only one tripe shop, from Norfolk Street all the way down to Church Walk, and everyone liked tripe. This tripe shop was run by a lady called Mary Grief, and it was very popular, as it was spotlessly clean and very hygienic.

J.P.

We used to make toffee

I still have my mother's handwritten recipe book. We used to make toffee with brown sugar, water and vinegar boiled in a round heavy cast-iron pan. You dropped a teaspoonful in a saucer of cold water and if it rolled into a hard ball it was ready. Mam would sell some to Fulwell schoolchildren and those going to the Marina cinema in a piece of greaseproof paper for a penny. Cinder toffee was made by adding a teaspoon of bicarbonate of soda so it frothed up. I liked the lemonade made with fresh lemon juice and sugar and water boiled up and bottled. It had to be diluted to drink it and we put a pinch of bicarb in to make it fizzy.

A.B.

A wedding in the street was always a great event

A wedding in the street was always a great event. The whole street would congregate round the gate waiting for the bride to appear and a cheer always went up when she did. It was the custom for the bride's father to throw a handful of coins out of the bridal car for the children in the street to scramble for. During the war years, neighbours would give up food-ration coupons to help out the bride's mother with the catering.

M.R.

My mother used to have a round oven

We lived opposite the school and those other children that lived a distance away used to bring cans of tea or soup and a pie and have them cold for their dinners. My mother used to have a round oven, old-fashioned round black oven, you know, with a coal fire. She used to put the pies in the oven or the soup on the hob to warm and to give them it at dinner time. They had to warm them you see. She used to make toffee on a Sunday night and sell it through the school railings at halfpenny a packet, you know.

S.N.

It tasted great and was very filling

In the 1950s I lived in Monkwearmouth and recall that when times were hard the women would get together and each would give an ingredient to make a broth. It would be cooked in the copper boiler where the cloths were washed and when done would be shared out among the families. The main ingredient would be sheep's head, fish or pig trotters together with the vegetables. It tasted great and was very filling.

C.W.

I asked the wife to cook sheep's head broth like me mother

When I was married in 1958 I asked the wife to cook sheep's head broth like me mother. I had to tell her to cover the ready-sliced head with cold water in a big pan and boil for, well, ages. To skim off the scum then add chopped vegetables (carrots, turnip, potato, onion) barley, salt and pepper. I went out. I didn't know she didn't know how to serve it. She had seen pictures of medieval banquets with a pig's head on a platter in the middle of the table so she did that! It looked.... 'orrible. She was supposed to strip off the cheek meat, cut out and slice the tongue, remove and mash the brain then serve it all neatly on a plate with the vegetables. We had a few more

Narrow Flag Lane, High Street, Sunderland.

done properly, but she complained about the persistent cooking smell and finally refused to do any more. BSE stopped the sale of sheep's heads and she said, 'about time anyway. It's foul. I wouldn't do it for the dog now.'

M.T.

We thought we were the bee's knees

One of the funniest days of my life was when my friend and me went to Seaburn. We thought that we were the bee's knees. We had our high-heeled shoes on, our swagger coats and our hair was piled higher than the Tower of Pisa. I had run out of hair lacquer so I used sugar and water. Walking proudly along the sea front, one or two wasps appeared, buzzing above my head. Then it seemed like their brothers and sisters were joining them. It was time to run! You could have heard our squeals a mile off. A lesson was learned that day: do not put sugar on your hair.

O. H.

Men were wearing the Edwardian look

Clothes were rationed from 1940 on a kind of points system. Each person had a set number of coupons to last six months and every garment had a value. We had between thirty-two and forty coupons and even towels, sheets and knitting wool had a value. A pair of shoes needed five coupons, a skirt seven, and a coat twelve. During the forties fashion was about saving fabric, as you may imagine. The garments in the shops were cut with the idea of saving every scrap of fabric. Skirts were short and slim and jackets were fitted. In the late forties, when the fashion industry was again operating without constraints, we saw skirts dip to mid-calf length and the full-circle skirt also became fashionable. Hats went crazy with swathes of chiffon tied under the chin. Men were wearing the Edwardian look, which had them dubbed Teddy Boys and clothes altogether were more lavish.

A.M.

The south end of Sunderland railway station.

Our local bobby

The police in those days were respected. Our local bobby was called Big Jack, and he was big – nobody upset him, but if you were in trouble he'd be there to help you. I had a slap on the backside from Big Jack when he caught me throwing stones. I didn't tell my folks because I would have got a crack from my dad, as my dad's answer would be if Jack gave you a slap you must have done something wrong, as he was held in such esteem. He was around between 1955 and 1962.

C.W.

That special time in history

In 1953 when the Queen was crowned, we all had parties in the streets. A few of the streets had their own Queen, all dressed up in a long white dress and a red cape. I was the Coronation Queen for Henry Street and Henry Street East and had six attendants. On Saturday, we all paraded around the town while the crowds of people clapped and cheered. The schools too, had celebrations, Hendon Girls School had country dancing in the schoolyard. We all got a coronation cup as a keepsake of that special time in history.

A.H.

three

Leisure

Having lifebelts was never thought about

In 1944 I was in the Sea Rangers with skipper Elaine Flowers, (sometimes called behind her back as Buncha), meeting in All Saints church hall in Fulwell Road. We treated the hall as if it were a boat with a red port light and a green starboard light rigged up by Jimmy Flowers with the flag being hoisted and lowered to the sound of the 'bosun's pipe'. In 1946 the boat SRS *Delhi,* built by Dugdales, was launched and we spent many exciting hours down the North Dock. We had only four oars as skipper felt six oars were too heavy for young women. We wore quality, hard-wearing ex-Wrens skirts and jackets from the Army & Navy Store. On the boat we wore white, square-necked shirts and navy trousers with white covers over the hat in summer. Having lifebelts was never thought about. I rose to the rank of petty officer.

E.G

It was the twenty-fifth anniversary

It was the twenty-fifth anniversary of the Rangers, and a rally and parade were planned for spring weekend. As accommodation was hard to get in London, especially at a price young people would be able to afford, it was decided to make the deep air-raid shelters available to us… There were very basic toilet facilities and areas where hot drinks could be prepared but they were very deep underground and the stairs had to be climbed, as the escalators had not been fitted… On the great day the sun was shining and we were instructed to wear our white shirts and navy skirts, together with our hats. We wore the flat caps issued to Wrens and bought at the Army Surplus Store, and we carried navy-blue jerkins of the kind issued to air raid wardens, again from the surplus stores, as they did not require clothing coupons. All was fine until it began to rain and we put on those navy jerkins. The dye soon washed out and into our smart white shirts. It took more than a drop of rain to dampen our spirits though. After the parade our group of about sixteen girls, looking like drowned rats, adjourned to the Hyde Park Hotel – an extremely upmarket place – and ordered tea and cream cakes. To our amazement the very generous cakes were filled with lashings of fresh cream. We had not seen such luxury since 1939, but it seemed not everyone was in the same position as the Sunderland folks; some were more equal than others. Back home on the night train from King's Cross, so ended that adventure.

A.M.

Crystal Palace rally, 1948. The Girl Guides.

Buckley family and friends on the beach, 1940s.

Seaburn, Sunderland, 1920s.

Exciting, horrible screams

I was a starting member, (aged ten), of All Saints Girl Guides in Monkwearmouth in 1928. One night we were sitting in the dark round a 'fire' made of sticks, red paper and a torch, singing camp-fire songs. The final song was 'A woman in the churchyard said', which always ends with exciting, horrible screams. Suddenly there was a loud banging on the locked door from a worried policeman who thought some terrible crime had taken place!

M.H.

Seaburn, Sunderland, 1929.

Everything was a child's dream

Seaburn in the 1950s was a busy place. The shops were full with children buying buckets and spades, sweets and ice cream. Visitors were sitting in cafés having tea or coffee in clear glass cups, writing postcards home. It had a great family feeling about it. On the beach were canvas huts and deckchairs for hire, on the far side of the road stood kiosks, painted, and draped to look bright and inviting, making you want to buy from them and people queued for the tea, chips, winkles and candyfloss they sold. The music coming from the fairground kept the holiday feeling going all day. The screams coming from delighted children on swing boats and walzers, bumper cars and roundabouts. Everything was a child's dream.

K.C.F.

My first job

My first job was to accompany my dad to his allotment for a head of lettuce (sandwiches in the hungry '30s) while dad checked and watered his allotment and mam made the sandwiches, I set off for Seaburn with the dog to meet my cousins and claim our usual spot. Gradually all my cousins and aunts and uncles arrived and my mam and dad with my younger brother. 'Our spot' was a rock just in front of the old tram terminus. It was all in the fun for uncles and older cousins to catch you and dump you in the sea. When the tide came in we would retire to the recreation park for a game of cricket or rounders.

After the war we moved along to the 'second shelter' towards Whitburn. Then our friends were marrying and bringing the next generation along. Dads took children down on the bus, while mams pushed prams down. When it was time to go home, mam went on the bus with older children, and prepared a meal ready for when dad arrived after pushing the pram home. By the next generation it was changing. Holiday camps and caravan parks were becoming popular and it wasn't too long before we were flying off to the 'Costas'.

T.B.

It was the custom on a hot day

My father was one of a large family and it was the custom on a hot day to meet on the beach. My father, brother and I caught the

Seaburn and Roker, 1930s.

Seaburn, Sunderland.

bus to Seaburn Camp at 7.30 a.m. We hired a tent and deckchairs and had fun erecting them. The whole family made a semi-circle on the beach and it became like a settlement. We spent the morning playing with cousins, but at 11.30 a.m. prompt we were at the bus stop to meet mum who had been at home baking pies, boiling potatoes and other goodies for the picnic. We built sand tables and had our teapot filled at the kiosk. What a feast we had. A wonderful day was had by all, and all for the cost of the bus fares.

D.S.

Tropical island paradises

The beach was between the Toll Bar and Ryhope Dene, taking in the Ryhope Village Beach. The stretch of beach from the Toll Bar to the village at that time was over a lovely golden sand. Families used it for picnics and paddling, swimming etc. It was marvellous until they started to remove the sand for building purposes. Between the Toll Bar and the village was a point jutting out which was known locally as Hill Sixty. When the tide came in it was possible for the more adventurous of the lads to dive off the end of the point… Another memory which comes to mind was a lovely Friday afternoon; the beach beside Hill Sixty was deserted and I had just come out of the water after having a swim. Where I was lying on the sand was a suntrap. It was wonderful lying there, it made me think of tropical island paradises. The most hateful thing was I had to go to work at the pit, Ryhope Colliery.

S.H.

Some of my very first memories are of the Illuminations

Some of my very first memories are of the Illuminations. The lights would be on

Illuminated tramcar at the Roker Gala, 1902.

throughout autumn and as a boy I'd love nothing more than to wrap up warm and look at the displays, explore the Fairy Dell and gaze in amazement at the floating tap in the boat pond. It would be years before I worked out how they made it appear as if it was suspended in mid-air. The atmosphere around the park was one of excitement and, as I made my way down to the magical caves by the beach, the sweet smell of doughnuts wafted through the air. The lights stretched from the harbour view to South Bents and if I was lucky, one of my grandparents would drive me along the sea front as the matchstick boxers, basketball players, footballers spanned the road, capturing my imagination as we drove under each set of lamp-posts.

A.S.

Holey Rock, Roker, Sunderland, pre-1914.

East End carnival possibly. Thompson Builder float.

Health and safety would have hysterics today

The landmark event (of the Model Boat Club in Roker Park Boating Lake) was the Illuminations every year. We put on a three-day event. There was an exhibition marquee filled with model boats, where some hardy volunteers slept overnight and yes, it was always cold, often wet, but never miserable. During the day the public could sail our boats, but at night there was the set display. A 12ft-long model coaster packed with fireworks would leave harbour only to catch fire and blow up, breaking in half. Sirens would blow and a child selected from the audience would launch a lifeboat down a slipway. Tugs would retrieve the two halves. The PA system would carry a running commentary. There would be five performances a night. Health and safety would have hysterics today! They were great days but sadly unrepeatable.

E.F.

The East End had a carnival every year

The East End had a carnival every year, which would be led by the jazz bands or ragtime bands. They were mainly unemployed men, as from 1930 onwards there were large queues at the employment exchange. My uncle was a member of a group who named themselves 'The Rudolphs'. They made themselves black sombreros, stitching medallions round the brim, and wore red shirts. There was only one women's ragtime band, named the 'Spanish Ladies'. Sampson Besford, the strong man of the area, would pull a lorry along with his teeth; also they would smash bricks on his head. There was a tug of war staged, but naturally the team who had Sampson on their side always won.

At carnival time there would be a fairground, which covered all the Town Moor. The whole community got together; also it gave the unemployed something to do, to make the carnival work. Each street had its own street party and all the exterior of the houses were decorated. It gave the people in the area an identity and pride in what they could produce.

W.D.

She used to poke lots of sheepish-looking couples out of the shadows

When I was about seventeen I started going to Weatheralls, which was a dance hall somewhere in the vicinity of the carpark behind Debenham's. I remember a lot of old houses in the area of The Green and that was where it was. It was run by two (I think) ladies, who I thought were old at the time, and it was more like a church hall than anything else, but it had a lovely bouncy floor, and we met lots of nice boys in there. Up above there was a sort of balcony which overhung the floor below, and it was dark under there, with forms to sit on at the back, and I clearly remember one night one of these ladies going round with a very long pole, which she used to poke lots of sheepish-looking couples out from the shadows.

J.G.

I can't remember going to a pub at that age

I used to get the bus home and at Boldon Colliery. In the evening we used to visit the Boldon Colliery Picture Palace quite frequently. The films used to be changed three times a week and we enjoyed that… sometimes you'd go out with a boyfriend. Sometimes you'd go to a dance. We used to get the bus into Sunderland and there were picture houses and The Rink ballroom. I can't remember going to a pub at that age. In the summer we used to go to Notariannis ice-cream parlour down the sea front at Seaburn.

C.B.

Many a romance blossomed

All the social life in Sunderland in the 1950s included dancing, especially at The Rink in the town and in the Seaburn hall. As a trumpet player in a local band I spent many, many happy hours playing for the young people. Fifty years later the dance nights are still talked about and many a romance blossomed as our music set the scene.

M.H.

Dancing cheek to cheek

I was seventeen years old – old enough to go to The Rink dance hall in Park Lane. This was with my parents' permission, (they were quite strict on where I went and who with). The Rink had a big band, led by Al Flush – he played the best music of the day, they didn't sell alcohol in dance halls – only soft drinks or cups of tea. The Rink was the most popular place, especially with the young generation. The Rink was my favourite; Saturday night out, didn't finish work until six o'clock, it didn't take me long to get ready. I remember wearing a full black skirt mid-length, tight short top, waspie belt and nylon stockings. Dance shoes were worn then – outdoor shoes, coat and hand bag were left in the cloakroom. My hair was short and curly with the help of curling pins, very little make-up (a bit of lipstick). It was mostly ballroom dancing – the tango, quick-step, waltz, not forgetting the barn dance… this one always had the floor full… After a few dances he might ask to take me home, this might lead to a future date or 'see you around'. Many met their life partners meeting like this. I met my husband at The Rink. We have celebrated fifty years of happy marriage.

Today's youth don't know what they are missing; girls dancing with girls and boys with boys. It was nice being treated like a lady and dancing cheek to cheek.

M.L.

I had a pair of Wellingtons

I usually bought my clothes from a second-hand shop beside St Ignatius church, Hendon. I think they called her Jenny. If she had anything special, like a nice dress at a cost of five shillings, she would keep it for me. I paid her weekly payments of either sixpence or a shilling. Mother once got me a dress made, one of the few new things, I think it was only two shillings. I had a lovely summer dress on and I hadn't any shoes. I had a pair of Wellingtons. I had to wear them. It was a hot summer's day. We met boys by going up High Street, walking around Crowtree Road and back again down High Street to the ice-cream shop where one night I met my husband.

B.S.

The best seats in the house

I knew the excitement of being old enough to go to the Ritz cinema on the corner of Holmeside and Park Lane to see *Gone with the Wind* – the epic film of its day – in the Regal in Holmside. For 1s 9d, you could be in the circle, the best seats in the house, with a variety act to entertain you while the reels were being changed. The Havelock cinema was at the end of Fawcett Street and the corner of High Street. Here tea was served on the balcony of the circle! On the corner of Bedford Street, close to Caslaw's men's outfitters and the Theatre Royal cinema was Joe Reay, huddled close to his hot-potato machine.

E.H.

Bridge Street, Sunderland.

The Ritz picture house.

We had great fun and all for 6d

During the late 1940s and '50s, all us kids went to the Saturday morning pictures. There were about four cinemas in the town that had the kids' shows on Saturdays and it was 6d to get in. If it was your birthday, you and a friend could get in free and sit upstairs. At 9 a.m. it would start off with a sing-song, followed by kids out of the audience getting up on the stage and singing or dancing. One girl got on the stage almost every week and sang 'Mares eat oats and does eat oats'. We then had cartoons, a serial and then the main film. We whistled and yelled at the villain, the lads all rode imaginary horses if there was a western on. Hopalong Cassidy and Roy Rogers were our idols. We had great fun – and all for 6d.

A.H.

The Havelock Picture Hall, Sunderland.

We could go to the pictures for a penny

On a Saturday we could go the pictures for a penny, and we used to go to the Bromarsh and, if we had tuppence, we could go in the best end – this might sound snobbish but we would look down at the penny-enders. At first it was the silent films, and when the words came on everybody used to speak the words out loud… There were forms for the penny end, and you got scrushed onto the forms, and that was what we called the penny scrush. The… Bromarsh was bombed during the war, and there were a lot of houses down Bonnersfield and people living just past the Bromarsh, when it was bombed, never got out.

J.C.

The Cora de Lop

During the war I saw wagons with chimneys on being driven up Southwick Road. They made smoke clouds to hide the docks from the bombers. On Sundays, all day, there was a 'thump, thump, thump' from the Doxfords

The Sunderland Empire.

The Cora Picture Palace, Sunderland.

engines being tested up the river. After going the messages, on a Saturday afternoon I used to go to the Cora cinema at the Wheatsheaf, sometimes called Cora de Lop because there were so many people with fleas. Most of the men were away so most of the people were children and women who used to shout, 'oooh! Look at that', 'Gerrim!' at the screen. If the reel stopped they would stamp and chant 'ugh, ugh, ugh' and Markey would bang his stick on a bench while yelling 'sharrap, sharrap. I'll hoy youse arl out'. It was frightening going home up Southwick Road in the dark after watching *King Kong*.

I.R.

At the Milly
My memories are vivid of the late 1940s. We, as kids, were regulars at the Milly, (as we affectionately called the Millfield) – often going twice a week… there was always such a long queue. As I recollect, the entrance was a small door in Hylton Road, near the railway station, along a corridor to the pay box. You went down narrow stairs into the cinema and the seats at the front were benches. We were packed like sardines but still we were asked to move along – often, the end one fell off. Mr Prior was the manager; a very nice fellow. A checker, Lamby, was a character and everyone knew him.

Each night we saw a main film, a small film or cartoon, and the news (no one had a television then). It was during the war, with news of bombings etc in our town and other parts of the country. I don't remember there being X certificates. We as kids saw horror films that would be adult-only now. As I left school and was courting, it was a cheap night out at the Milly. Upstairs, of course – real seats.

The Winter Gardens, 1941.

A few sweets, bought at the corner shop, not the inflated prices in today's cinemas and it was nice and warm on a winter's night. Not far to walk home to St Mark's Road, too. No tram-car fare. It didn't cost much for your night's entertainment. We were happy and content with our simple pleasures.

M.L.

The Winter Gardens

The Winter Gardens was also the place where all the old men from the East End used to congregate. Also in the gardens, there was a parrot and the bird used to pick up all the language from the old men and used to swear like trooper, which reduced my mother and her pals to hysterics. Sadly my mam is now frail, both physically and mentally, and only has her memories.

A.S.

St Ignatius had a boating club

St Ignatius had a boating club; we used to go to Girdle Cake Cottage… This was a boating trip; there was a boathouse and we had two boats – all the church institutes had boating clubs in those days. There use to be a regatta. It was held down on the Ravens–Wheel Course near Castletown, near Wearmouth Bridge, the north side of the river. The lads would fly up and down and cheer their crews. The race would be a measured distance.

E.H.

A grand time was on Easter Monday

A grand time was on Easter Monday when young people would go to the quayside and hire a rowing boat. We could get as far as Biddick, stopping on the way to have a picnic or games. Someone would take a melodeon

Sunderland Mission to Seamen's boat.

Ferry Boat, South Hylton, Sunderland, 1948.

or a wind-up gramophone, or even a mouth organ. We had to know all the tides because if you didn't get back to Claxheugh Rock before low water you had to get out then drag or carry your boat to deep water. There was no water at low tide. But that was all part of the fun.

T.H.

A favourite Easter outing

A favourite Easter outing – when lots of people, young and old, would go to the quayside to hire a rowing boat for a day on the river. We could row up as far as Biddick. We would soon reach Hylton Woods, a lovely area, also a favourite camping place for Boy Scouts or anyone who liked camping. There was a little stream from which we made our tea (it was good clean water). At another spot approaching Coxgreen we could land and walk up to Penshaw Monument, or rather climb up – it was very steep!

We would choose a spot on the riverside or field to have our picnic tea with plenty of room for games and entertainment. We always managed to have either a wind-up gramophone or a melodeon, even a mouth organ. Time soon

The Victoria Hall, Sunderland, 1938.

passed and the return journey was much harder when rowing back. We all arrived very tired at Panns Bank landing steps where the ladies disembarked. Us chaps went on to the Low Quay riverside, where the owner of the boat we hired was waiting. All at the end of this perfect day – had a great time.

T.H.

A penny was quite a big find

All the church institutes had football teams and badminton, table tennis, (well it was ping-pong – it wasn't called table tennis in those days)… the subscriptions were certainly very low – I should think it would work out not more than a penny a week. Your average pocket money was probably three pence to six pence; a penny was quite a big find. We used to have dances you know, for Christmas, Easter and New Year and other times, perhaps some special effort. We danced at one time till twelve o'clock at night… and the one they had at Burlington Road was always very well run. There was always keen competition for people to get tickets, because they were always sure there wouldn't be any drinking.

M.H.

Many young people met their future partners there

The highlight of Sunday nights was going to Victoria Hall's Sunshine Meeting. Of course, the main attraction was to meet the opposite sex. For after having a real good Sunshine singing we would flock out and make our way along Fawcett Street, up High Street along Crowtree Road and into Park Lane then on to Mowbray Park. We would then do the whole walk back again, boys chatting girls up and vice versa. Many young people met their future partners there. These walks were known as the 'Monkeys Parade'.

T.H.

The world-famous Roker Roar

I remember going to Roker Park on the 27 February 1973 as a fifteen-year-old schoolboy to see Sunderland play Manchester City in an FA Cup fifth round replay… On this occasion the pre-match pints and banter had been cut short by the world-famous 'Roker Roar'. The crowd really was at fever pitch by the time the gladiators entered the arena. The chanting, singing and encouragement was said by older fans who attended this pulsating match to

Sunderland, FA Cup winners, May 1937.

Sunderland football team, 1951.

be the best they'd experienced – even better than the FA Cup tie with Spurs in 1961 when Ireland skipper Danny Blanchflower stated he'd 'played all over the world. But I've heard nothing like the Roker Roar.' Many of our players were frightened – the hairs on my neck were bristling in fear.

T.L.

I was initiated into the world of football

I would do my shopping in town on a Saturday afternoon then get the tram home and this is when I became aware of the interest shown by the women of Sunderland in their local team. I was amazed to hear the conductor being asked, 'do you know what the score is, bonnie lad?'

The answer would either bring a big smile or a long face. You see, the tram was driven to Roker then turned round and came back to the town, this way the conductor always seemed to get the latest score which would then be passed on to the passengers.

It was also on these Saturday home-match days, that I first heard the famous ROKER ROAR. You could hear it whereever you were in Sunderland, or so it seemed to me. This sound, which usually meant a goal had been scored, became very familiar to me over the years and no doubt sometimes put the fear of death into their opponents. I vividly remember the year Sunderland won the cup by beating Leeds – what a celebration was had by all.

M.P.

The building of the Stadium of Light, Sunderland, 1996.

The demolition of Roker Park football ground, 28 February, 2002.

The pitch sloped a canny bit

I went to Hood Street Methodist Sunday School in the late 1930s, where Mr Barrass was the lay preacher acting as minister. He was a proper old-fashioned dedicated man, who had a big influence on hundreds of youngsters and always had a full house. He lived in a colliery house in Wayman Street in Monkwearmouth and his day job was in Fulwell quarry. I played football for Hood Street team in Thompson Park where the pitch was uneven and sloped a canny bit, but we just got on with it.

M.T.

Drama productions developed

A boys' club in the 1930s used the cottage attached to the Methodist Chapel on the corner of Fulwell Road and Atkinson Road. They moved to the abandoned air-raid warden's HQ on the site of the present Fulwell Library and Ebdon Lane. The HQ was demolished about 1950. A youth club was formed in 1948 and met in the chapel cottage. Drama productions developed. They got better and better, especially when the new chapel and spacious hall (with stage and curtains and that), were built in Seaburn Dene in 1961.

The Avenue Theatre, Gilbridge Avenue, Sunderland, 1932.

Our annual full-length Christmas pantomimes were a major and very popular feature for the area until the final one of *Pinocchio* in 1998.

R.M.

Then ask the dog to pick a domino

He (father) also had a black Alsatian-cross that he taught to do tricks in pubs. The plot was to walk into a pub with his dog, and anyone that was playing dominoes, he would say shuffle those dominoes up and then pick one out and give it to me, which they did. He would then show everyone the domino, then, put it back in with the others, then he would say, 'give them a shuffle', they would shuffle the dominos and then ask the dog to pick out the domino. The dog would always pick up the right domino in its teeth everytime. Everyone was amazed at this trick. But it was quite simple – the dog

would only pick out the one that my dad had touched, as it got the scent off his hand, when he showed them the domino.

T.P.

My favourite was the escapologist

I remember going to town with my parents. My father had the funny idea that going to town when the shops were closed was the best time of all; but my mother did not agree. It was however, a family outing. We always ended up in High Street next to the bomb site – which is now Argos – and smaller shops. Here, there were entertainers and salesmen trying to earn a few shillings extra. My favourite was the escapologist with his chains and sacks. I was very impressed and never once saw him stuck. Near him stood the man selling whelks – which I was never allowed to buy. Years later, when I was allowed to go to town on my own, whelks were to be my first purchase, including the pin. Imagine my disappointment when they turned out to be revolting.

D.S.

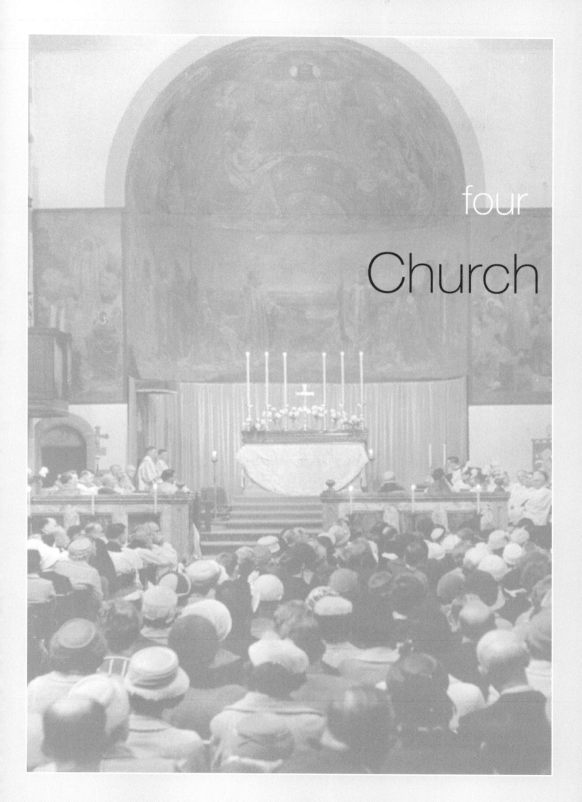

four

Church

Home and Family Mission Team, Venerable Bede parish, 1954. Venerable Bede church at the Wheatsheaf.

Venerable Bede's Mission. Max Thompson and the choir boys, 1954.

He always wore his long black cassock

Venerable Bede church, at the Wheatsheaf was Anglican, sometimes called high church with candles and incense and, in the 1950s, the vicar was Fr Gus Curtis. He always wore his long black cassock, even in the street, with a flowing black cape. He used to join in all church-group activities in the Jeffery Hall in Monk Street with the curate, Birman Nottingham, and a deaconess called Miss Wallace. She wore blue church garments. In 1954 there was a mission team from Mirfield. The leader was Fr Hoey. We all joined the youth club and the choir. The main one from Venerable Bede's was Max Thompson who became an RE teacher and also a church reader. By the mid-sixties the beautiful church was closed and ran for a few weeks under Revd Lacey-Jones from St Peter's. He moved on and Venerable Bede's was eventually demolished. Members dispersed. Some were lost to church-going altogether and a Kwik Fit car repairers' business was put on the site.

P.D.

I played Judas

In the early 1930s, St Peter's Hall, in Dame Dorothy Street, was the venue for many memorable occasions. In one Passion Play, I played Judas and closed with the words, 'I go down into hell, where the worm dieth not and

Silver Street, Sunderland, Holy Trinity church.

the fire is never quenched,' with a rope tied round my neck. When I was three visiting the ancient St Peter's church seemed a long walk past a high stone wall to see the flag of St George flying in the graveyard, which loomed on the left of the slope. At the far end was the mortuary. When I was seven and joined the choir, I had to be initiated by spending at least fifteen minutes in the mortuary or I could be put in a tomb. They said they would slide the lid back and put me in amongst the bones!

J.C.

I always had somewhere to go

A Mrs Whittaker used to teach us children at a sewing class on a Monday night, which I attended with my friend. I also went to the Seaman's Mission if there was a concert. Every Sunday morning I went to Sunderland church. I was all over as a child. My father would always ask me, 'where are you going tonight, pet?' It would be the Quaker church or the Bethel church in Villiers Street. They would have a little concert every week, it cost three pence and we got some lovely entertainment. This was the way I spent my life when young; going to different churches with my friends.

Miss A.

The bombing of St Thomas'

Of course it was bombed and Mr Orton was the last vicar we had and he and his wife one night thought they would go up in the gallery and they thought about an air raid I suppose. They had a building in the gardens, you know... So anyway, there was one night Mr Orton said to his wife, he said, 'I think I'll go upstairs and watch in case the bombing starts'. So she said, 'well I'll come with you and bring Paul (that was their son)'. So anyhow, they went upstairs.

Of course, the way I know so much about that little episode – Mr Watson the organist and Mrs Watson were our oldest friends. So anyhow, they both went up with Mr Orton and they'd been about two hours and he heard planes. Now he said, 'I feel very unhappy, go downstairs and I'll follow you'. Well anyhow, Paul and his mother went downstairs and he'd just got down when the place was blown up and, of course, they were all killed. That was forty years ago.

Miss A.

A lot of us met our future husbands or wives there

A crowd of us all went to Fulwell Methodist youth club in the early 1950s. We gathered in the premises, a cottage in Atkinson Road attached to the Chapel. We played games like table tennis; had beetle nights and socials where we danced the barn dance,

A church outing, c. 1900.

St Bernard's waltz, gay gordons and dashing white sergeant. We had regular bus trips to Whitley Bay and Whitby. All these meant we had plenty of opportunity to mix because we all went to single-sex schools. A lot of us met our future husbands and wives there, like me. Later a new chapel was built down the road at the new estate of Seaburn.

L.E.

We also had the Bethesda Mission

We also had the Bethesda Mission, at the bottom of Millum Terrace, which my sister and I went to. Mr Bell was the supervisor there and it was a clap-happy thing. There was a Miss Beck there. I can remember her closing in prayer – she was always asked to close in prayer... If there is anybody alive today that went to the Bethesda, they will remember Christmases there. All the toys were on a rope, right up in the ceiling, and when Santa came in, they pulled the rope down, and you were waiting for your name to be called, because there would be a present with your name on. It was a wonderful, wonderful time.

As we got older we went to St Peter's. There was Miss Dagg, and Edie Jopling – I knew these people very well. I was involved in something every night, there was a 'girls' friendly', and we used to go round to the mission hall in Dame Dorothy Street. You name it, we were in it; we never walked the streets or anything. We did a lot, there was the Roker, and the King's Messengers, the Girl's Society, and Edie Jopling and Miss Dagg used to take us to all these different things.

J.C.

The chapel has been gone a long time now

During the late fifties/early sixties, my friend Pamela Willis and I went to the Sunday

School at the Independent Methodist Chapel in Ryhope. It was an old stone-built chapel situated at the bottom of Ryhope Street. Once a year there was a Sunday School anniversary, it was held in the summertime and was always a great event – to us anyway. On the Sunday morning a couple of the men from the chapel carried a little organ around the streets, together with a party of chapel folk. We would stop in certain places and sing a hymn. One of the men would shout out the announcements of the afternoon anniversary and a few of the older boys and girls would collect money, door to door in a tin. In the afternoon we would all be decked out in our best clothes, eager to say our pieces that we had learned by heart and happily sang the new hymns. The chapel has been gone a long time now; a row of council bungalows stand where it once was.

M.L.

They were two separate factions

Bishopwearmouth church at this time was very low church. The congregation was very divided in so far that people either went to the morning service, or the evening service: they were two separate factions. There was a gallery round the church, which the young people preferred. The main body of the church was full, especially the evening service – people even sat on the stairs. If there were a vacant seat then the churchwarden would ask older people if they would go down and take the seat, therefore nobody would migrate down into the body of the church until they were asked. There was always a full house. Unfortunately there was a decline in numbers after the war, owing to the houses in the vicinity being demolished and not replaced, and the birth of the council estates.

Mr L.

Hooper Street Mission

[It] was half the size of Bishopwearmouth Hall and situated in a down-town area, namely Johnson Street and Johnson Court, also tenement houses and warehouses. The mission was packed each Sunday. The reason for this was because the people from this area felt their clothes were not good enough to attend church. I was christened at St Mary's Mission. Mother held my christening back as she thought St Andrew's church would be completed, but it was a few years later before the new church was completed. I think mother's ambition was for me to be one of the first to be christened there. Anyway, I was in my early teens when I attended St Andrew's.

Mr L.

I am H.A.P.P.Y.

During the late 1940s and early 1950s, everyone went to Sunday School. I went to the Gospel Hall which was also known as the Tin Chapel. The excitement of the week was a Tuesday night when they put on a lantern slide show. The church was always packed and the more friends you took for the first time, gave you a star on your card. After a few weeks, the one with the most stars got a book. Then there was the Sunday School treat – that was once a year. Off we all went on a bus, sometimes it was to Houghton, where we had races and such like on a huge field. We came home on that day, tired but happy. Christmastime brought the anniversary – we all learned a piece of poetry or sang a song. Mums and dads used to come along to listen to their children. We sang some lovely choruses at the Gospel Hall, there was 'I am H.A.P.P.Y', 'Down at the bottom of the well' and 'Jesus wants me for a sunbeam'. They were happy days for us all.

A.H.

St Columbus', Southwick.

Sorley Street Congregational church outing to Ambleside between 1905 and 1910.

Pilgrim Street Methodist Sunday School annual outing to Hylton Castle, early 1930s.

Above Gilbertson's pawn brokers shop

My great-grandparents were Roman Catholics and lived in Camden Street, Southwick. At the time there weren't any Catholic churches in Southwick, so my great-grandmother used to go collecting for the church, asking them to buy a brick each week. I do not know how long it took them to collect the money for St Columbus church but they held services in little rooms above Gilbertson's pawn broker's shop in Southwick Road: this was where St Columbus' church was founded. My father was twelve years old when the church was opened and he was one of the first choir boys. The curate was called Hornsby. He became a bishop in Africa and would come back to St Columbus' every anniversary day. He would enter the church in his bishop's robes and hat then sit on the throne. My father used to take a full orchestra to play for the service. Today St Columbus' is a very high church.

Mr L.

I couldn't see any mercy in her, like

I started St Hilda's Roman Catholic School in Southwick when I was five, and Sister Eucary was a little angel – everything you could imagine a nun to be. Sister Edith was, like, head of the infants – strict but not too bad. Sister A was head of the seniors – and she was really bad. One time she brought in this little tot, about eleven. She says, 'Mr Waller, this boy has not been eating properly in the canteen. Give him four of the best!' and left. Mr Waller was a gentleman. He says, 'put your hand out', tap, tap, tap, tap. But she'd been watching and she made him hit this tot again, hard.

Another little lad came in dirty and she gorrim in front of the class. She purra dish o' water down and pushed him across the desk and give him a real good scrubbing. Aw, y' know, we thought it was horrible. The sisters wore their habits and were called the Sisters of Mercy, but I couldn't see any mercy in her, like.

The sisters used to come round every week to collect money but when I stopped going to church Fr Mulligan came and says to me mam, 'ho! You'll come to a wicked end' and she says, 'you'll come to a quick end if you don't gerrout,' and there was no more money after that. Sister A used to walk round the streets sometimes on the night and if she saw any of the girls and boys the next day she would growl, 'Yous girls will end up on the streets and yous boys will end up on the galas' [gallows].

G.H.

There was all the usual things

Well, there was all the usual things, Sunday School, youth clubs on Tuesday in the old Burlington Road Institute… that had been a mission hall that had started before St Ignatius had come into being. You see, it grew from there. Apparently, I believe it was from seven to eight, and the lads used to have gymnastics and then at eight, the girls came as well. We used to dance till ten on an ordinary Tuesday night. They put on concerts, amateur dramatics and things like that… And of course it was a great missionary parish, there was always King's Messengers and King's workers, [for] which we used to have Bazaars. We used to do missionary plays as well. They had a boating club at St Ignatius, which we used to go on the river to Girdle Cake Cottage on Wednesdays and Saturdays. There was a boathouse and we had two boats…

M.H.

The church also held film shows

The family attended Herrington Street Methodist church, which unfortunately is no longer in the Hendon area. My father was in the choir and attended the men's institute in the winter evenings, playing billiards mostly. My mother played the piano for the Sunday School. The big event each year was the Sunday School anniversary, which was held in June. A tiered stage was erected in front of the pulpit and children recited, sang solos and sang as a choir. It was a big occasion as I was bought two new dresses each year plus a new pair of shoes. The prettiest dress was reserved for the afternoon service as the children had a much larger part in this service.

The church also held film shows. The films were mainly Charlie Chaplin with a religious one thrown in which you watched in sufferance. You queued for hours to get in, so as to get a good seat, which was usually sitting on the windowsills as you were high up and no one would block your view.

D.L.

Magazines in a buggy

As one of eight children I was taken to St Peter's Sunday School when I was three. And when I was twelve, confirmation classes were in the vicarage in Bridge Street, facing Monkwearmouth station. There was a mission hall in Dame Dorothy Street used for everything St Peter's organised. For many years Miss Dagg would pull magazines in a buggy to deliver to everyone in the parish. The Sunday-School teacher was Mr Davison with Miss Davison, and Revd Hawke, as well as Miss Dagg, used to collect children like the Pied Piper on their way. At Christmas we were told to sit on the floor for Father Christmas to come with his sack. Father Christmas was the Revd Hawke and one boy was in trouble because he shouted this out! Sadly the mission hall was bombed during the war, then we moved to the national schoolroom nearby and events went on.

J.G.

He really worked very hard for the poor...

He [Canon Hedley Jackson] was a very forceful preacher and when he got really going he sort of ignored the stammer, but he had this very bad impediment... as long as he sang

Sunderland Seamen's Mission, 1905.

things he was alright... He organised tramps for the men when they were unemployed. They used to go up to an old school in Middleton, in Teesdale and it was very cheap for them, and some of them had never had holidays like that before. He really worked... very hard for the poor. And when the women were going on trips he used to get on his own motorbike and go ahead and took them on mystery tours. He would go ahead of the bus, you see, and they would have to follow him and they never knew where they were going but he always took them to some very nice little spot...

M.H.

A muffled bell

When Queen Alexandra died the church bell in the town were muffled and rung at the day of her funeral. But, two or three days before this our chief bellringer at Bishopwearmouth church, a Major Robert Hudson, (he had the ironmongery shop just round the High Street from Church Street), took it upon himself to muffle the bells. He lived quite close at hand in Church Lane. He informed his sister where

he was going and what he was going to do. Later on in the morning they heard a muffled bell come down but thought nothing of it. As time went by and he had not returned home his sister went to see the verger of the time to go and see where he was. Unfortunately the verger reported he had been killed in the belfry. The very large bell which he was muffling had come down and jammed him in between – I forget what you call – them between the outer bell, the hammer and the bell, which was very heavy.

Mr L.

And the visions went

My family were not Jehovah's Witnesses and when they knocked we always just closed the door. One day, when my little girl was two, I was feeling horrible because she was a restless demanding baby and my husband was depressed and my uncle had just died not very old. In fact I seemed to be having delusions like a body hanging in the dark coalhouse (probably because of lack of sleep). Anyway, when the Witnesses came that day somehow

Sunderland parish church, from Church Street, Sunderland, 1950.

I couldn't shut the door. They gave me some leaflets about wicked spirits to read and when they came back they talked to me about my troubles. They told me to pray to God and call him Jehovah: his personal name, 'ask for what you need in Jesus' name'. I did this and the visions went and the baby settled down. I went to Bible study and the meetings in Kingdom Hall in Toward Road. I got baptised and held home meetings. Jesus said, 'go from door to door in twos and preach the Good News', but I only did that for a while.

A.T.

A Sunday School treat

When we lived in Deptford we had a Sunday School treat. We use to walk from Ayres Quay Mission to Millfield station, we went from there to Cox Green. It was only two stops away and you would think we were going to Hong Kong – hanging out of the windows, waving away in the train. We would get off the train and march to the field. We would get tea, a bag with sandwiches in and a snowball, a bag of sweets, as many cups of tea as you liked. 'Course our mams went with us. We use' to play races.

P.W.

A number of Jewish pupils

In the early 1950s Bede Girls Grammar School had quite a number of Jewish pupils who all had to leave early on winter Fridays, because they had to be home when their Sabbath began at dusk.

S.P.

A hive of activity

Dock Street was one of three long streets, which was divided into three blocks. Dock Street Methodist church was in the middle of the top block, on the left-hand side going down towards the North Dock. The church was a hive of activity in the 1950s. There was the Girls' Guild and the Greenwoods on Monday evenings, Boys' Brigade Tuesday evenings, also Christian Endeavour for the adults. Bazaars were held in the junior rooms. Every Sunday afternoon, children ranging from three to fifteen could be seen making their way towards Dock Street for Sunday School meetings at the church. Sunday School treats would be Lumley Castle, Saltwell Park or Crimdon Dene. These trips were the only time some of us got to venture out of the area.

The teachers of Dock Street were an inspiration. There was Miss Hetty Cuthbert and her sisters Molly and Matty; Mrs Learmouth; Miss Lauterbach (a German family who had a Lemonade Factory in Zetland Street); Mrs Butterfield; George Potts and Revd Lewis Allison. Older women did not like the children to play any sort of games on a Sunday: it was a holy day. When my friend, Linda, and I came back from Sunday School we would sneak into the house and get our skates and go out to play, but somehow Linda's nana would find us and we would get into trouble. The church and the teachers were a good influence on our lives and made us into better people.

M.T.

My Sunday School did not march

I remember going with my family to watch the Good Friday march. My Sunday School did not march, but I was dressed like the rest of the young girls in my new dress, blazer, hat and brown Start-rite sandals, and taken to watch. We stood in Fawcett Street in front of the balcony of the town hall, and sang hymns. Following this, we and the rest of our extended family went down to Coronation Street to Sans Street Mission for a short service. Then we walked up High Street, calling in the shop for our fresh fish, then called into Notarianni's

San Street Mission, Sunderland.

for an ice cream. Lunch must have been very late on Good Friday in those days.

D.S.

It wasn't all just hymns

I was born in Grangetown. On a day when I was four years old, I decided to follow some children into this hut. It wasn't like a church from the outside; it was called Miller's Mission. There was lots of children in and they all seemed to be having a good time, but it wasn't all just hymns that you sang, there was games and trips organised. We used to go on trips to Cox Green and have picnic lunches and things like that. It was run by the Miller family who lived in Grangetown. There was two brothers and three sisters. Nobody in my family went there; they used to go to other churches. My sister and two brothers used to go to the Wesleyan Chapel. I wandered about from church to church... On Sunday mornings I went to Saint Aidan's church, which is a high

church. I was confirmed there, but I still always had this thing about Miller's Mission.

Well, I think all children should be taught religion – I don't think today children goes to Sunday School. I wanted to go. Well, you learn what's right and wrong.

M.P.

I'm not a pacifist

I'm not a pacifist. I'm a conscientious objector actually. A pacifist doesn't believe in war for any reason. We believe in God's war against evil, because 2 Corinthians 10:3 says; 'Though we walk in the flesh we do not war in the flesh'. So our Christian warfare is a spiritual one, not a fleshly one. My father-in-law was sent to prison for a year for refusing to fight. He was fairly treated there. Some Jehovah's Witnesses did go in the Army but they would not carry arms or kill. They were very brave on the battlefield as stretcher bearers.

B.S.

Revd Martin Turner and the fire damage at St Peter's church.

I had a lovely warm feeling come over me

When I was married I took my children to Sunday School at the Methodist Hall, at the top of Thorney Close, as there was no church on the estate. Later I moved to Silksworth. When my daughters had grown up they took me to see Billy Graham at Roker Park football ground in 1984, where people were asked to go forward. I had a lovely warm feeling come over me and I went forward. Later a member of North Street Wesleyan Methodist church invited me to attend there as he had seen me go forward at the Billy Graham rally.

M.W.

We had three mandolins

I was born on 1 January 1906 at 57 Coronation Street, opposite the church on the corner. When we were young we went to a Catholic church, but later on we turned Protestant. When I went to the Catholic school we had school trips. They had a St Patrick's club where they played billiards and cards at the top of Coronation Street. That's all there was. Well, we played football for St Patrick's school every Saturday morning 'cause me big brother played for the big team. St Patrick's team, they used to play on the town moor, St John's church and others.

I went to the Hebron Tabernacle in the High Street – used to be the Seaman's Mission – I never went to church regular. I used to go sometimes when I had to go to confession. But the trouble was they marched you from school into the confession box. The priest in there asking how many sins I had committed in the week. Well, I thought this is all wrong, not right at all, not according to

A fire at St Peter's church in 1984.

the Bible, because I read the Bible everyday. I was thirty when I started to preach the Bible, preached the Gospel like Billy Graham; salvation through faith. There was four of us and we preached around Hendon, Millfield, East End, sometimes out of town, Newcastle.

We had three mandolins when we sang some lively choruses; the congregation also sang. After the session we would stand up and give a sermon about Christ and salvation, then there were prayers. Sometimes the congregation would be would be seventy or eighty. The little colliery places there would only be about twenty or thirty. We never took any money. Those in charge sometimes passed a plate round. We never had any money and paid our own fare on the bus and train.

S.Mc.

Three weddings and a funeral

I have always had a passion for church organs so I was overwhelmed in 1962 to be appointed organist at St Peter's, Monkwearmouth. Built in AD 679 the ancient site housed a wonderful, famous Wilson organ; it was a privilege to play. Every session I spent at the keys was special and once I played for three weddings and a funeral all in one day! Then in 1984 a deranged man set fire to the church. Flames leapt high, smoke and ash gushed everywhere destroying much dry, wooden timber and we lost the altar, the vestry and it broke my heart when I saw the priceless old organ reduced to ashes. After many hours the firemen had put out the fire and saved the stone walls, the pews, the landmark tower and the ancient original glass from Italy. In the end a meeting room,

Left: *Steven McGuinness with his brother; both were Pentecostal travelling evangelists. They preached on the Town Moor.*

Above: *James William Street Chapel, Sunderland.*

the Chapter House, a visitors' area and a new altar were built. A replacement electric organ was installed. It cannot compare at all with my beloved Wilson organ, but I can still make music in a special, heritage setting.

I.N.

company and stayed after school for meetings. This kept my mother happy as it meant I did not need to go out after dark to go to a Guide meeting. At the same time we had blackout restrictions, which were very strictly enforced because of the danger of air raids. I was a member of the church youth group which met in the clergy-house and, as this was only a few hundred yards from home, my mother saw no problem in me going there.

A.M.

Leisure time as a teenager

Leisure time as a teenager was spent in a variety of ways with some variation according to age and one's interests. I believe a higher percentage of young people attended some form of worship than is the case today, and there were many church-based activities in which we took part. As a thirteen to fourteen-year-old I was a member of the school Guide

five

Schooldays

East End school scene possibly. Drill or dancing...

I loved my little bottles of milk

I vividly remember starting Chester Road Infant School. It was September 1966. I quickly fell into the rhythm of the school day, and looked forward to the little bottles of milk that we were given. The bottles were usually carried, clinking in the crate, into the classroom by the two milk monitors. The crate was left until our teacher decided it was time to drink it. Then, and only then, while seated at our desks, the monitors would hand out our little bottles of milk along with a wax-coated paper straw. It was very important that the straw was treated carefully, as you were never allowed a second one, no matter how flattened and soggy it got. I loved my little bottles of milk. It was the highlight of my day. But winter turned to spring, then summer and oh, how the milk began to take on a sickly, off taste. The smell was quite nauseating. I decided then and there that I did not like milk after all, and have never drank it since.

C.C.

Be quiet!

I stayed at the Middleton Camp, age fourteen, in 1946 with my own friends in Class Three General in West Southwick Boys, for a week. The teachers were Tashy Hylton, Dan Walton (PE), and a third, who all stayed in their own room at night except to come out and shout, 'Be quiet!' West Southwick had a good football team and played matches organised by the teachers against the village lads who we thrashed ten-nil. We took packed lunches on walks, played games, wrote home for more money to spend in the village shop and had no lessons. We travelled on a hired bus. My friend Bruce Winter went too. I also went to Seaburn Camp for three days. I slept in bunk beds in the Army huts, played football on the beach and in the field. We went on a trip to Marsden.

S.C.

This bloomin' great bull came thunderin' at us

I went from the National School in Monkwearmouth to Middleton Camp. Because me da was workin', I had t' pay fifteen shillin's for the week, which was a lot o' money in them days. The teacher said, 'Remember. If you cross a field the animals are more frightened of you than you are of them so just keep going' – eeeeee. We went into this field full of cows and kept walkin' like she said and this bloomin' great bull came thunderin' at us! We ran like anything scatterin' pies an' all sorts. My friend hurt her back on the wall and how aa gorrover that fence aa'll never know t' this day!

Mrs C.

We made bunks in woodwork

I lived in Pallion and went to Havelock Secondary Modern School. In 1950 we made bunks in woodwork to be used by the schools in Middleton Camp. I paid £1.50 at a shilling a week to Mr Robson to go on the steam train with our class of thirty boys and three teachers. From the station we walked to the camp, carrying all our gear packed in kit bags.

Boys doing woodwork; learning a new trade.

We went to a sheep auction and saw all the sheep up for sale. We took the bus to Cauldron Snout and walked back. Our sandwiches were made by the kitchen staff.

J.H.

I stung my legs on nettles

Middleton Camp 1987 from Monkwearmouth Comp. I stung my legs on nettles then jumped in ice-cold water. We told scary stories of the Blue Lady and Mad Monk, then dared each other to go to the toilet near the exit, at night. The teachers slept in another room.

J.M.

A visit to Middleton Camp

Generations of Sunderland children have spent a week in term time at the council-owned Middleton Camp, in Teesdale. The bus trip was in an old bone-shaker, with much [out-of-tune] singing and several cases of travel sickness. Oh, the delights of settling sixty boys into the dormitory. First night; last boy goes to sleep at 8 a.m., first wakes at ten past. No sleep for us teachers.

…Walks in the rain dressed up in red water-proofs – 'one size does not fit all' – like a flock of dispirited penguins, strung out along the road, the teacher bringing up the rear (me) the most dispirited of the lot. First major walk round Falcon Clints to Cauldron Snout was enlivened by the discovery of the egg of the lesser-spotted weegie bird (hard-boiled and lovingly decorated the night before!) The trail of corned beef and tomato sauce sandwiches were left behind for local livestock. Swimming at Fairy Dell, (the fairies were always out). Many wondered how they turned the waterfall off at night. The visit to Barnard Castle saw some homesick charges phoning and imploring parents to come and get them! The inter-schools cricket and football fixtures continued until the midges ate the umpire. I will never forget those midges. Finally the frenetic tidy-up on Friday night, brought the discovery of a breeding colony of socks behind the radiator. Home with thoughts of sleep and on Monday morning greeted as I entered the staffroom, 'did you enjoy your holiday then?'

E.F.

A visit to Middleton Camp. Swimming at the Fairy Dell.

A Middleton Camp expedition.

I've never tumbled my creels since…

I was at Cowan Terrace Juniors and I had just passed my eleven-plus exam to Bede Girls Grammar School in 1947 when I had the chance to go to Seaburn Camp for a week. At the time I had long curly hair, so before I could go to camp my mam had to treat my hair with Suleo [a white emulsion] so that I wouldn't end up with dickies [nits]. We slept in a dormitory in one of the old Army huts. One corner was partitioned off. This was where the teachers slept. Early morning there was long queues for the outside lavvies. There wasn't many of them. Meals weren't up to much either. Breakfast was a doorstep of bread and a ladleful of baked beans. No butter. Two cooks sliced each loaf with a two-handled saw.

We had outings but had to walk everywhere. On one day we walked the field path to Whitburn parish church. I discovered what fossils were that day. They still fascinate me. Another day we went to the waterworks. The pump was very big and shiny. On return to camp we had to write a composition about the visits. We spent time at the beach. Sitting on the prom, we had to draw Roker lighthouse and the shipyard cranes. We then explored the rock pools. I didn't manage to dislodge any limpets but enjoyed popping the seaweed. Back at camp we had to paint our pictures.

Any pocket money was spent at Hastings shop at the end of Sea Lane, next to the Seaburn Hotel. One evening, when the teacher was out of the room we started larking about. I tumbled my creels on the bed and something went wrong. I opened my eyes to see the teacher looking down at me and lots of faces round the bed. I've never tumbled my creels since!

We went home having enjoyed ourselves but the highlight of each day was when our mams landed after tea to talk to us through the railings!

R.T.

We had cold water wash

Whinlatter Pass in Braithwaite, near Bassenthwaite Lake is where we went from Sunderland in 1935-36 with Mr Robinson, headmaster and three more teachers… Arriving at the station there was a Boy Scout-style barrow to put our kit on and pull it up the bank in turns. Camp was a wooden hut with a kitchen, a dormitory with straw palliasses on the floor. We had cold water wash. Cost £1 for a week. There is still a camp there (modern).

M.A.

It really was educational

I was one of the pupils at Bede Grammar who joined other schools for a cruise on the ship *Devonia* in 1964. We visited Heligoland, Copenhagen, Oslo and Poland. Mind, the North Sea crossing was so rough I was seasick out and back. We sat huddled in a group on the top deck and I was so ill I just wanted to die. We were issued with sick bags we had to throw overboard after use. Visiting the Tivoli Gardens in Copenhagen, we were fascinated by the lights and music. We sniggered at the nude statues in Norway and I thought the vast Holmkollen ski jump used in the Olympics was awesome. The seaport Gydnia in Poland was a very drab place.

Walking round the ship was difficult. Moving from side to side you had to find your sea legs. We slept in bunk beds on the lower deck. The dining area was on the lower deck as well and the smell of the food made me feel sick again. It was my birthday on board and my name was called out on the morning tannoy system after the wake-up call. Evening activities included dancing to Lulu's hit 'Shout!' We wore school uniform on shore but shift dresses were all the rage on an evening. I think this was an inspired opportunity from the council. It really was educational.

M.H.

Bede School Sunderland, now part of the City of Sunderland College.

While strolling in a crocodile

In September 1973 my class from Seaburn Dene Primary went to local authority Moor House for a school field trip. It was my first time away from home, so excitement was running high. I used a black and white camera for the first time and entered my snaps of 'imaginatively focused' Finchale Abbey into Mr Whan's school photographic competition, winning a prize! While strolling in a crocodile… for nature study with Mr Finney, I spotted a discarded Villa pop bottle. With the deftness of the current Sunderland's FA Cup-winning hero Ian Porterfield I booted it – straight into a concealed wasps' nest, screw top first. A swarm of angry, disturbed wasps emerged, the orderly crocodile scattered in all directions, and my good pal Gary Johnson was stung all over his face and hands… He reminds me of this sorry event every September!

N.T.

Unlike the majority of my contemporaries

I had taken the eleven-plus examination and transferred to the local grammar school in September 1941, so unlike the majority of my contemporaries, I was not expected to leave school at the age of fourteen, but to continue in education for at least a further two years and sit the School Certificate Examination. Afterwards I would have the choice of leaving school to enter the civil service, a commercial office or some similar job, or remaining at school for a further two years to study for the Higher School Certificate. Gaining BSC meant it was possible to go on to college or university. Only a small proportion of young people did this. Those going to university were still predominantly the offspring of the more wealthy members of the community.

A.M.

Boys doing PE at school. East End Orphanage.

Bede Girls Grammar School staff in 1960. Front centre is Miss Moule.

Slates to pens

I started school in 1930 at the old Colliery School at the Wheatsheaf, less than half a mile from Wearmouth colliery. After one year that school closed although the buildings are still there. They have been converted to small industrial units. All the children formed a 'crocodile' and, with their books under their arm walked... to Grange Park – a newly built school. From the nineteenth to the twentieth century in fifteen minutes' walk. From slates to pens and exercise books, even radiator heating instead of coal fires. Even some younger teachers... We even had flower beds around the playgrounds. I particularly remember the quadrangle, whose borders had been sown with Nasturtium seeds for the first year in new soil.

T.B.

Don't be cheeky lad, pits or yards?

In 1963, having failed the eleven-plus... I started Grange Park Senior Boys School... The teachers were of the 'old school', very strict and with plenty of forms of punishment – mostly the cane but with an odd slipper here

and there, and they all had a good story or two from their days in the Army during the war. The headmaster was Mr Morrison. Mr Dixon and Mr Johnson taught woodwork and technical drawing, Mr Stafford taught maths and art, Mr Potts geography and music, Mr Sanderson history and PE. Mr Chicken taught science and Mr Topliff poetry and english – his cane was called 'the little yellow god' which lived in the locked cupboard.

In my last year at school, one thing I can remember is an interview with the careers officer on his annual visit to the school. 'Pits or yards?' he asked me. 'I want to be an electrical engineer,' I told him. 'Don't be cheeky lad', he said. 'Pits or yards?' I left school in 1968 to serve an apprenticeship as an electrical engineer at an engineering firm in East Boldon.

D.B.

A cloud of lavender perfume

The headmistress was Miss Moule when I went to teach German at Bede Girls Grammar School in 1950. She was passionate about her girls, going round the building in 'floaty' outfits, in a cloud of lavender perfume. Eventually she retired and Miss Bradbury became head. When the comprehensive system started she was appointed head at the new-built Pennywell and I went too. I found it challenging to teach mixed classes, but I liked the spaciousness of the place and enjoyed being with such lively young people.

M.D.

Excellent, dedicated teachers

In 1948 the Council decided to convert Monkwearmouth Central School in Swan Street to a grammar. In 1949 I was one of ninety eleven-plus passes, boys and girls who went to mixed classes there…We were kitted out in navy blue. Berets for girls and caps for boys topped blazers with no badge or braid as the other grammars had. Bede had blue and St Anthony's green. In 1950 Bert Lomas, the art teacher, designed our badge. It had St Peter's church in honour of the Saxon monks and a sailing ship in honour of Sunderland's great shipbuilding industry. Below entwined M.G.S was a motto 'Crescat Sapientia' meaning, 'let wisdom increase'. Marjorie Waite, deputy head, chose purple braid to edge the blazers. The Swan Street building had many physical deficiencies, but excellent, dedicated teachers, with games on the field at Thompson Park and Wearmouth Colliery Welfare. Newcastle Road baths saw our school produce many very talented swimmers. In 1963 everyone moved to the wonderful new building with its own fields and swimming pool in Seaburn Dene, by then the start of the modern comprehensive system.

M.A.

I went to Monkwearmouth

I went to Monkwearmouth Grammar School in 1956. I seem to recollect these teachers. Stuart Wilson was headmaster. Fred Purnell taught Latin — *surgo ambulo revenio sedeo* was the first lesson in form IB in Swan Street. Mr Frith and Miss Bagley took sports. Stan Buchanan taught history. Mr Clough taught Geography. Marjorie Sparling taught RI. Miss Thelma Swan taught French. Ben Tinker taught woodwork. Ralph Lowe and Chic Young taught English. Miss Marjorie Suffield taught chemistry. Mr Halstead taught maths. I was a member of Newton House and gained colours for swimming, rugby and chess. We all ended up as prefects! I've still got a school blazer (now split up the back) with the MGS badge on.

D.D.

Annual galas were an exciting event

Physical education at Grange Park Junior and Secondary schools in the 1940s onwards was in the parquet-floored main hall with small balls, hoops and skipping ropes. The wireless provided dancing to music classes. In the schoolyard we could race, play cricket and football or go up to Thompson Park and kick about on the rough pitch there. We walked to Newcastle Road baths for our swimming lessons and the annual galas were an exciting event to which the whole school went, and some national competitors emerged as a result.

P.D.

One of my freshly cooked dumplings

I remember the fun we used to have during domestic science lessons… in the early 1970s. There was always a mad scramble to get to the kitchen furthest away from Miss Montgomery's desk. The additional benefit to bagging a place in this kitchen was that the door handle used to stick and could only be opened from inside. This gave us the opportunity to mess around whilst waiting for our mince and dumplings and apple

Grange Park Junior School gala at Newcastle Road swimming baths, c. 1972.

Washing, ironing and mangling – daily chores.

Monkwearmouth schoolgirls embarking on the Nevasa *for a 1964 Baltic cruise.*

crumble to cook – much to the annoyance of Miss Montgomery, who used to rattle the door handle, demanding to be let in! I particularly remember one occasion when a friend dared me to throw one of my freshly cooked dumplings at her. Being in a particularly mischievous mood, I took up the challenge. Although my aim was good, she quickly ducked and the dumpling flew out of the window, landing on the head-master's car! The usual shrieking and laughing ensued, followed by Miss Montgomery banging on the door. Fortunately I was never identified as the dumpling-throwing culprit!

S.D.

I can remember the early days at school

I can remember the early days at school, you know. I don't think I was even in what they called the baby class, but I remember one teacher bringing a dog to school – it was a big St Bernard dog and she used to leave it about her – and another time I remember we had a concert at school and we were giving a demonstration with dumb-bells, you know little children, but then one of the rooms had a gallery and when I was little I was moved into this room with a gallery – I can remember coming home at dinner time and saying

Possibly Hudson Road School, 1930s.

to mother, 'Oh! I'm bigger than the teacher now, you know'. Oh, we had lots of happy times…

Miss B.

'BOYS' at one end and 'GIRLS' at the other

Starting at Grange Park Secondary Mod. in 1973 I stood looking at the brickwork, reading 'BOYS' at one end and 'GIRLS' at the other. The big bit in the middle was the main entrance with two great big bay windows looking out to the yard and high railings. Once inside the mainly square glass window-walls on the corridor side of the classrooms could be slid along to open it all up. In the centre was a surprise garden with a pond and summer frogs and hundreds of brilliant coloured nasturtiums.

All the classrooms had huge blackboards that spun round on a roll-type system cleaned with wood-backed rubbers that often became missiles when there was no teachers about, dust flying all over. The end room near the toilets was the lab. In the biology classes we used bunsen burners and once built a wormery to watch them working. The teacher would hand out sheets, hand-prepared and printed in purple ink from a spirit duplicator because we hadn't many text books. When you did well she gave us a handwritten note signed and dated. It was exciting to make simple recipes in cookery to take home in a covered wicker basket, with a fitted plastic cover – the 'in thing'.

D.F.

Today you are going to swim

For several decades from the late 1950s the family of Bagleys was renowned in the educational circles of Sunderland. In September 1963, after passing my eleven-plus exam, I was pleased to start at the new Seaburn Dene site of Monkwearmouth Comprehensive School Phase I… This new building was, I believe, the first in Sunderland to have its own swimming pool, which was the pride and joy of the PE mistress, Jean Bagley, whose objective was to have every female pupil able to swim within the first year. Towards the end of that year she was very near to achieving her goal with only me and one other pupil, Evelyn E., still unable to swim. One day the fearsome Miss Bagley took Evelyn and me up to the side of the deep end and said, 'today you two are going to swim.'

I was first. She took my hand and then pushed me into the water! Down I went and up. Down I went and up. I remembered my dad saying to me, 'if you go under the water three times you are drowned,' so I thought, 'I'll have to swim', and I was so terrified I did. Evelyn was even more terrified than me, and when Miss Bagley held her hand to push her in she couldn't leave go and pulled Miss Bagley, fully clothed, into the water with her, much to the delight of all the pupils and making a heroine of Evelyn. Thank you, Miss Bagley, I actually still enjoy swimming today.

A.G.

I'm the school board man…

I went to Green Terrace School – that was the easiest of course. The reason I went to Green Terrace School, my cousin and I – in those days you had to, there wasn't anywhere to play or things like that; you had to play in the street. We were going round and round the lamp-post, when this person come and said, 'Why aren't you at school?' We stood there dumb-founded, you see. So he told us, 'I'll go and see your parents, I'm the school board man. How old are you?' We must have been five years old and he saw my parents and my cousin's parents and the next thing was up to school, Green Terrace School: that's how we started school. From Green Terrace School – but in the first instance, Green Terrace School had a juniors

on the ground floor, infants on the ground floor and then they had a senior section. From there you were transferred to Cowan Terrace School, which of course is now non-existent of course because that's on the same plot as the Civic Centre.

Mr L.

I can still do a mean hem

At Grange Park School during the war the baby-class teacher was Miss Dippie, who taught us letters on sand trays and slates. Next was Miss Patterson who did some simple hand sewing with boys and girls. Miss Whale did 'land drill' with us. We lay across forms to prac-tice breast stroke before going to Newcastle Road baths to actually swim. Once I was sent back to school for being naughty. I bought a bun and an Oxo to crumble in it and ate it on the way back. Miss Humphrey terrified me with her threat of the strap, but I loved the art stuff, copying the colours in an autumn leaf with pastels, making regular squared pat-terns with paint, and keeping silkworms. Mr Common, newly returned from the war, had a military ability to humiliate but also involved us in a lot of different singing presentations. Miss Blackman, with her ringleted locks, did more advanced sewing. I can still do a mean hem. We did tests every week and sat in the order of our results. When I passed my eleven-plus I was allowed to run home after assembly to tell my mam.

S.P.

Glass scattered everywhere

I was looking out of the window in lab room thirty-two one dinner hour in 1979, as a new appointment at Monkwearmouth Comp. I couldn't believe what I was seeing. The mas-sive, whole glass wall of the swimming pool fell out in slow motion and crashed onto the concrete quad. Glass scattered everywhere. A girl had simply leaned on it; the last straw after thirteen years of warm damp air slowly destroying the wooden frame. It was screened off for weeks before the gaping hole was completely bricked up.

S.T.

There were forty-eight children in the classes

As a student teacher at Langham Towers in 1940, I was sent to James William Street School (Jimmy Willies called locally). We were warned that some children were stitched into their clothes for the winter and they couldn't take off any for PE. They must have gone to bed in them and they never got washed. Soon after the war I was at Havelock Infants. Ford Estate hadn't been built long and all the houses had bathrooms for the people coming from the East End slums. One little boy came everyday dirty. He said, 'we keep the coal in the bath.'

Another said they kept a donkey in the bathroom because it was downstairs.

Nurse 'Nitty Nora' never came to us, as every child had lice and fleas. My mother would comb my hair with a toothcomb over a newspaper on the table and once I squashed a creepy crawly which fell out of my hair onto the register. We tried to control them with a weekly wash with Derbac soap because the white specks stuck on hair near the scalp are eggs, which can't be killed until they hatch. There were forty-eight children in the classes and once I looked after two classes with nearly 100 five-year-olds for a few days until a supply teacher could be found.

E.H.

We couldn't use anything

In 1968, when I was five, I was at Redby Infants School and had to travel there from Seaburn Dene on a special bus. I once got wrong off my mam, for leaving my new woolly trousers on the bus and I never got them back. Six

The Gray School, c. 1916.

Thomas Street School staff, Sunderland, 1957-8. Turpin is the third from the right in the back row. Silvia Thompson (nee Phillips) is standing on the left.

months later a new school had been built just in front of our house and I went there where Annie Sanderson was headmistress. All the schools were teaching us to read by ITA (Initial Teaching Alphabet) and it was hard learning to read and write and spell in proper English later on, especially as we couldn't use anything except the school books.

A sentence in ITA: 'wee ar aull helpig too mxk a bonfier.'

N.B

The most important item was the rocking horse

Miss Lazenby was the first teacher the five-year-olds would see on starting Thomas Street Infants School. Her classroom was at the end of a very long corridor. On entering the classroom the most important item in the room was the rocking horse, which every child wanted to play with first. Miss Lazenby would tell us that while we waited to get our ride we could play with the sand and water. This scion made us forget that this was our first day at school and put all the small children at ease. When the children became seven this was the time to move into the primary class. The infants of Thomas Street just moved into another part of the school where they were joined by Stansfield Street schoolchildren. Everyone soon made new friends.

M.T.

If anyone didn't pay attention in his class

Mr Alan Turpin took the 4B class [at Thomas Street Junior School]. If anyone didn't pay attention in his lesson he would throw a piece of chalk or a net ball at the child. This would soon bring the child out of her or his daydream. He could hold most of the class' attention most of the time, and often told humorous jokes. He once said that in our lifetime (the year then being 1957) we would have no jobs and the collieries and the shipyards would cease to exist. This brought a great cheer from the class, especially the boys. Little did we think this would happen. He then went on to say that we would all take up leisure activities, like jogging and keeping ourselves fit. He would take the class for music lessons. Everyone really enjoyed this lesson and the songs he picked were always full of vigour. In 1957 Mr Turpin entered the class in a song festival and the song he picked was 'Bobby Shaftoe'. By the time he showed the class how he wanted it to be sung, we sounded exceptionally good. Mr Turpin made sure we had spelling tests every week and was always giving the class homework, mainly things we would have to look up at the library or in encyclopedias. I liked Mr Turpin.

M.T.

Someone hit my sister with a sand pail

I remember starting Grange Park School at the age of five. I had a twin sister called Connie to share my fears and excitement with, though sometimes I wonder if that was a good or bad thing, because I remember one day at school someone hit my sister with a sand pail, so I waded in with the shovel from the sand pit. The teacher Miss Carr only saw my dirty deed, and I was quickly introduced to the back of the blackboard. I seemed to have spent more time at school behind the blackboard than in front.

Inside Middleton Camp.

We did all the walks

M.O.

When I was at West Park Central School I went to Sunderland schools Middleton Camp where we had to sleep on wooden trestles with a mattress on. During the day the ones in the middle were folded up and the ones round the edges left up. Sometimes someone, for a joke, made it so when we sat on one it collapsed. I expect the teachers did the cooking. We did the preparation, set tables and washed up. We went into a smelly hut to peel loads o' potatos and the toilets were outside. A highlight of the week was to go to the Cosy Cinema. So we gorall 'v our chores done. Great! Line up. All walk down. Oh no – it was closed! One time we went into the teacher's bedroom and purra brush in the bed. We hid outside and waited. The teacher screamed and ran out swingin' this brush! All exaggerated in good part for a laugh. We had to do a concert and 'cause I had long hair, I was volunteered to be Lady Godiva. Two girls were a horse. When they stumbled I fell off into the audience of children and teachers. We did all the walks including Kirk Carrion, which was a lot of trees beyond the house. We walked up this hill to get to them. We went to Cauldron Snout and High Force. One day we had a mouse and we had to gerra trap. We had to go each day to see if it was caught.

J.O.

Hudson Road School.

Hudson Road schoolchildren playing.

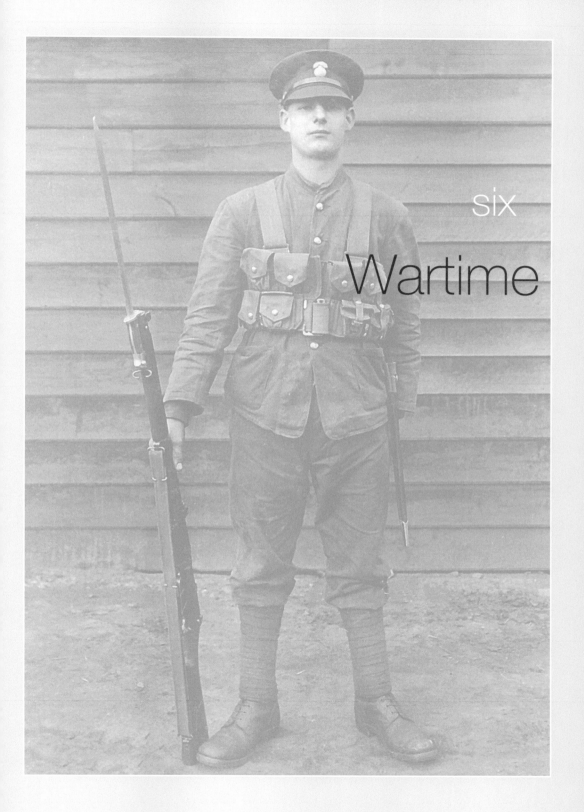

six

Wartime

Above and below: *The peace procession, Hylton Road. Sunderland, 1919.*

We didn't know war was serious then

I remember very well the day war was declared. It was Sunday morning, eleven o'clock. We were chased into the kitchen, so the parents could listen to the news. We thought it was funny and me younger brother got a clip for laughing. We didn't know war was serious then. We knew nothing about war.

E.B.

We knew them as neighbours

Coronation Street, in the East End of Sunderland, had an Italian ice-cream shop by the name of Puce's, which had little booths where you ate your sundaes. The family had a daughter who would go round playing the barrel organ, which us children loved. There was also a sweet shop at the top of Coronation Street run by a German family. When the 1939 war broke out and they were took in for internment it was ever so sad; we were all stood around as they were taken out, but it

Above: *Binns Store, Sunderland, 1941, after being hit by a bomb.*

Below: *Binns Store, Sunderland, 1949.*

wasn't because we were bitter or because of them being Italians or German: it was because we knew them as neighbours.

W.D.

It was the air raid sirens sounding

So I was about six when war broke out. It was a fine day, and the thing I remember most about it was the air raid warning sirens sounding, 'cause we had one just over the road to us. That was the first time I remember hearing them. They must have tested them when they put them up, but I don't remember hearing them then.

J.K.

It's my calling up papers

The most upsetting thing to me was me father was going to go away. I can remember even though being so young and still see him sitting at the tables with this paper in his hand and me mother being upset. He was saying, 'there is nothing I can do about it. I've got to go, its my calling up papers, I've got to go', and realising me dad was going to go away and leave us.

M.C.

Our air-raid shelter

The man on the wireless stopped speaking, my mother put her arms around me with tears on her face and said, 'God help us all, especially all you children'. My da dug a big deep hole in the back garden and our neighbours were doing the same. This was for our air-raid shelter. We were to use that often, mostly at night. It had four nice bunk beds in, a light, a little stove and a few tins of meat, soup etc. Some of our neighbours' shelters were not so good, built of brick; many were flooded with water. Over the top of our shelter my dad put soil, rocks and flowers, so from a distance it just looked like a big rockery. Sometimes if the

men were at work the women and children would gather in one of the shelters and we would play games like I spy, cards-snap and sing songs. In the door of the shelter there was a slit like a letter box and we would watch for the search lights in the sky and listen to the noise of the planes, which were ours and which were the Germans.

M.T.

Pets' sedative pills

People were not allowed to take pets into the public shelter I believe, although I'm sure some did. We had a cat who never seemed too upset during a raid. It would go under the bed or we would put it on our lap in the pantry where it would probably go to sleep. But dogs could get very upset and hysterical. I think the pet product firms brought out a type of sedative pill for pets... but I imagine that could cause problems. Think of the panic. The alert goes – father chasing the dog around the house to try to get it to swallow a couple of pills. It must have been funny to see.

D.B.

The blackout was taken very seriously

The blackout was taken very seriously. Of course there were no street lights on. The buses and trams had masked headlights with only a slit of light showing inside the bus. Only perhaps four bulbs on each deck and these were painted blue, as were part of the window. It was difficult to recognise faces in the gloomy interior. Blackout shutters were made out of a thin wooden frame covered by thick brown paper. These shutters fitted tightly into the window frame so that not even a chink of light was seen from outside. People moved about the streets by using small torches shining on the ground. The lens of these torches had to be no more than one

Sgt Tom Howell at Madras, in 1945.

Sunderland ship-building. Women were brought in to replace men during the Second World War.

inch diameter, I think. We extended the life of the batteries by warming them up on the top of the oven.

D.B.

Whenever sirens were sounded

Whenever sirens were sounded we were lined up and walked into the air-raid shelter… great big underground bunkers they were. The head master would bang on a tin tray with a big spoon, to warn us to get in line. Infants went first, followed by the others, the fourteen-year-olds were last, all with our gas masks, 'the inevitable gas masks', on our shoulders. When it poured with rain the bottom of the case got wet, the mask fell to the ground, it was all dinted to bits. We had practices with the gas masks on, but we never needed to use them.

T.H.

They were terrible places….

When the alert sounded during the night, we would go into a pantry under the stairs if it was a heavy raid. Then during a quiet period in the raid we would dash out of the back door and across to the schoolyard behind our street to the underground shelter. Probably more than half of our neighbours would be in there. They were terrible places. Duckboards on the floor

because they were always wet. Long forms along each side, with just a couple of candles for light and very cold in winter. There was a chemical-type toilet at the far end…

D.B.

A king-size wendy house…

I also remember when there was an air raid at night my father just picked me and my mattress up and carried me into the air raid shelter, which was built in the backyard then deposited me onto a bunk bed, there were two. The base of the bunk bed was made with thin strips of interwoven metal. Also in the shelter was a single bar electric fire, this fire sticks in my mind because the shelter was a lovely place to play in during the day, it was a king-size wendy house. Anyway I must, for some obscure reason, have draped my dolls clothes over the electric fire: in turn, this must have been switched on before we went into the shelter – consequently all the dolls clothes were singed; they were made of wool. I was upset, so probably that is why it sticks in my memory…

D.L.

I remember dried egg

I was six when the war started and we were rationed. I remember dried egg; we used to get one egg book if you were lucky. I never tasted banana. We used to stand in long queues for oranges and if you didn't have a green book you didn't get them. Sweets: we didn't get a lot of sweets – mother didn't have the money. My favourite meal was dried egg, sausage, black puddin'.

M.P.

I often used to wonder how she managed it

It was hard for my mother to feed us on ration (as I lived with my family), but we always had something hot when we came home from work (I often used to wonder how she managed it.) For baby we were given cod liver oil and orange juice. Most babies were on national milk which was quite cheap (two shillings a tin). When my son was small he had a very large gas mask. He used to fit right in it…

A.D.

I had to bend down and snip it with my teeth

This Saturday morning I was with me Aunt Mary and we were standing in the queue in the Central Pork Shop, the man tossed the sausage on the counter and it had a glass standing up and a piece of sausage came through the end of the glass. I had a small bag and I pulled this piece of sausage and it was linked and it just wouldn't stop and I was pulling the sausage and putting it in my bag. At the finish I had to bend down and snip it with my teeth, because I would have had all the sausage that was in the shop. When I came outside, and we all got a pound of sausage each, and when I came outside me Aunt Mary give me a clip, because I should have told her that I had all the sausage in me bag and they needn't have bought any.

M.P.

Margaret Preshaw's father in the Second World War.

And after that we always ate our egg first

I had a cousin, she was the same age as me, and we used to get half an egg each on a Saturday morning for our dinners, we used to have sausage, black puddin', white puddin' and this half an egg and we always left the egg till last, because that was our favourite. This day the sirens went, so we all run out and went into the siren shelter that was in the back garden; when we came back the dog next door… had run into the house as we run out and had ate everything in the house that was left on everybody's plate and everything there was and after that we always ate our egg first…

M.P.

Stockings were in desperately short supply

In the war few people had cars and horses were still a common sight and there were still the Brougham carriages, with drivers wearing uniforms and top hats. Stockings were in desperately short supply so our legs were painted with gravy browning and a line drawn up the back with a crayon or pencil.

E.H.

Government orange juice

Me mam used to get government orange juice, for vitamin C, from the health clinic, in Dock Street Chapel. It was in a flat square bottle, like a medicine bottle, about seven inches tall and two inches deep. Thick and sweet, a spoonful a day was nice. She never gave us the awful cod-liver oil, unless it was mixed in with the orange juice and I never noticed. Some people used to get cod-liver oil and malt for vitamin D and iron. I went to John Street Clinic for teeth extractions by gas, but never had any drilling.

A.H.

Food rationing never bothered me

Food rationing after the war never bothered me. I never knew any other. Pom [dried potato] was all right and I loved the taste of sandwiches and omelettes made with dried egg. Sometimes, instead of orange juice, we got Del Rosa, rose hip syrup. The national loaf had to be fortified with calcium.

A.H.

It seemed… everything was rationed

It seemed as though everything was rationed, or in short supply, or quite simply totally unobtainable… There was a system which gave a person a number of 'points' to be used at ones own discretion for items from a list which included tinned sardines, dried fruit (when available), tinned beans and sweet biscuits. We were supposed to get one egg each per week, but that again was if they were available. One could choose to forgo the family egg ration and have an allocation of corn for poultry food. We had an allotment garden and kept half a dozen chickens. We did not give up the egg ration but we fed the hens on table scraps collected round the other members of the family and good grown on the allotment. Normally the hens were going to augment the meat ration but those birds were my personal friends and I never could bring myself to eat them!

A.M.

It tasted arl reet…

My grandmother lived downstairs and she could hardly see. One day she was making the rations last by chopping up potatoes and onions and carrots for broth when she cut up a bar of soap which she threw into the pan. The mixture frothed up with soap bubbles, but my uncle Bob said it tasted 'arl reet'! I used to go with her to the Blind Institute down Tatham Street and I saw people weaving baskets at the back while she collected her five bob weekly allowance.

A.P.

The first banana…

We always seemed to have enough to eat, but I missed things like oranges and bananas. I remember especially the first banana I had towards the end of the war. How thin I cut the slices to put on my bread.

D.B.

The main entertainment

The main entertainment was the wireless…

The Rose and Crown High Street West, Sunderland.

Listening to Tommy Handley in *ITMA* [*It's That Man Again*] and other comedy shows. We also went to the cinema and the Empire. If a raid started when you were in the cinema a slide was shown on the screen announcing this, but the show carried on. Only once did this happen when I was there, we went home. My father, several times every week, would go for a drink in the town centre. I think the pubs had a beer ration for the week, because he would tell us that when, say, the Londonderry's beer was turned off, everyone would dash over the road to the Rose and Crown where they had just put their beer on. If a raid started the regulars would sometimes go down to the cellar for shelter. Dad sometimes returned home in the middle of a raid by train, alighting at Pallion Station only 100 yards from our house. He would say they laid on the floor for the journey as the train was being followed by enemy planes looking for the shipyards etc.

D.B.

Concert parties to entertain the troops

Children from the Fulwell Methodist Sunday School held concert parties to entertain the troops. These concerts started as far back as 1943, when aerial bombing raids had finished on Wearside. Even so, soldiers to us children seemed to be everywhere and if you wanted a piece of [rationed] chocolate, then the ATS ladies on the barrage balloon bomb-site at the top of Mayswood Road near the chapel seemed to have endless supplies...

R.M.

We had gone full circle

I was at Redby Infant and Junior School... during the war. Each morning we would see smouldering craters where the day before had been happy homes. I collected bits of shrapnel after air raids in Duke Street and Roker Baths Road and we boys spent... time swapping pieces from our collections. At night my grandfather, James Hogg, a miner from Southwick, was based in the school as a fire-warden. My father, Lance, of Beatrice Street, was on duty as a special constable at Roker Park Football Ground in May 1943. He was killed there during an air raid, when spare bombs were discarded by returning German bombers. This changed our lives totally and devastated the family. Thirty years later I was appointed head master at Redby Juniors and one day I found myself reading in the school log-book about those war-time years. We had gone full circle.

S.S.

A mortuary... for the bombing raid casualties

When the war broke out, of course there wasn't the coal to put in the (public wash-house) furnaces, so it had to be closed down. My mam and all the family were still there, but we weren't very happy with the situation, because in the meantime the ARP had took over the running of the washhouses and had made a mortuary out of it for the bombing raid casualties... The first ever bombing raid was in Newcastle Road and my mam had to help to wash this young girl that had died in the raid.

J.C.

The year is 1941

The year is 1941, I am three years old. It's a late autumn evening and we are sitting at the fireside waiting for the sirens to inform us that the German bombers are on their way. At prompt ten o'clock the sirens sound and off we go into the only shelter in the yard. Dad, my uncle and myself go into the back lane to meet the other neighbours for a chat. Total darkness. Suddenly we hear the drone of the German bombers approaching the town. We hesitate. Out of the darkness the sky is brilliantly lit up. Scores of searchlights roam the skies looking for German planes. Suddenly the 'ack-ack guns' commence firing. The noise is frightening, but exciting. I have on my tin helmet as shrapnel begins to drop from the sky. Now the bombers are overhead, we race to the air-raid shelter. Tonight they have decided to drop incendiary bombs. I rush into the yard with father and uncle to find that three of these bombs have fallen into the yard and are spouting flames. We manage to douse the

flames with a stirrup pump which has been issued to every household. We are lucky that no incendiary bombs have fallen on the house itself. What an exciting night it has been, 4 a.m. and we are just going to bed.

R.D.

I was reading the Dandy

At that time we lived at No. 11a... Dykelands Road. It was Friday lunchtime in mid-August. I was reading the *Dandy* and eating my dinner at the same time. A Seymour's pork pie and pease pudding. Normally I would have 'got wrong' for that, but mum was very quiet. She said she had a premonition and I just put it down to one of them funny adult sicknesses... Suddenly we heard the sirens, 'Wailing Willie' and gunfire over Newcastle. Mum herded us towards our shelter next to the cemetery wall... We could hear the 'planes above us then a new whistling sound. Mum shouted for us to put our hands over our ears and the kids were crying. I didn't actually hear the bomb explode over the road. It was like a rushing express train – then silence. The shelter door blew off, then bricks and stuff began to fall. Heavy stuff first then soot and dust. But it was all in silence! I will never forget. Mum hugged us for ages and it must have been about ten minutes before I heard anything again. It was the air raid warden from next door. His 'tin hat' clanged on the shelter doorway when he shouted, 'Is anyone in there?'

D.B.

I don't think I will ever forget that number

If there had been a raid the night before, when we got to school next day it was closed, because the people that had been bombed out were using the school. So we went away, to have a look at the bomb damage, and collect

Anti-aircraft guns on Tunstall Hill.

shrapnel and fill the day in, probably having fights with our gas masks as well, which we carried all over on our shoulders, and we also wore identity disks on our wrists with our names on and our identity number on, and my number was FDUN54. I don't think I will ever forget that number.

E.B.

I can remember one thing mind

I can remember one thing mind, we didn't have time to get to the shelter... We were sitting in front of the fire. I had one sock on and I put the other on... I remember that as if it happened yesterday. I looked at Billy Robson, he looked at me. Next thing I knew... I must have been knocked out, how long for I don't know, but I didn't know what it was. It suddenly dawned on me we'd been hit like. I couldn't get my breath... in fact I thought I was choking. I panicked. I heard somebody say don't move him like, or this might come down...The next thing I knew I was in hospital... I lost some friends, but lost the best friend you'll ever have, your mother.

T.L.

They were covered in blood

I remember one night during the war. There was a massive raid by the German bombers and the ARP rushed us all over to the shelters. The girls who worked at the sauce factory round the back of Monkwearmouth pit came rushing in screaming. They were covered in blood! Everyone screamed with them till they realised it was tomato sauce from the sauce factory. The bottles had exploded over them. We thought that was funny afterwards.

M.O.

It was great to wave to them

When I was about three, I lived in Barrack Street and used to see the wartime British soldiers billeted in the barracks across the road. I used to sit on a little window seat in our attic room and look out of the sloping windows at the sea in the distance. When the German planes came over to bomb the docks I thought it was great to wave at them! During one raid our roof blew off and was given a 'temporary' tarpaulin repair which was still on when all these old houses were demolished many years later.

A.P.

Next days news

In May 1943, when I was eight, the war was raging and our Millum Street cottage was on the bombers' map. The previous month my eleven-month-old brother, Howard, had died of lead-poisoning from shrapnel-contaminated milk and, after a heavy raid, my mother's nerves in ribbons and my father soldiering, mam and I overnighted at our grandparents' Grindon home. Thus the parachute mines which destroyed cottages in Medley, Millum and Lime Streets and wrecked, without warning, the room we would have been sleeping in, were next day's news to us. A glass light-bowl suspended from chains and a large cherry-boy ornament were blown and smashed into Howard's cot which had not been taken down. That late May raid also blew out of the ground the buried remains in Bishopwearmouth cemetery of babies including Howard. Bearing our flowers, my mother and I were turned away by a man posted at the Hylton Road cemetery gate, never to return.

D.S.

Black arm bands

I can remember children coming to school with black arm bands on and you knew then, although you didn't say anything to them, that somebody in their family had been killed, but you would say to somebody else you know that sort of thing. At school once I can remember a ship down on the Hendon beach: I don't know whether it had been blown up from a mine. Well something must have happened because there were dead bodies on the beach.

M.T.

Everyone was glad to do their bit

By 1943 my son was old enough to start the nursery and I wanted to do my bit for the war effort, like all the other women. I started work at Joplings glass house, but I didn't like it, so I got work at Steels, we had to do men's work – a lot of welding [at] which I was quite good. Wages were paid on a piece-work basis. I loved the company of the other women. They were a good lot always singing and we looked after each other. Everyone was glad to be able to do their bit…

A.D.

There was no extra pay for overtime then

I remember in 1944 when I was seventeen, I started work in the L&N stores in Trimdon Street. We had rationing of food, clothes, sweets etc and they all needed coupons, which we had to count every weekend after work. They were checked by a senior member of staff then taken to the food office where they were supposed to tally with the figures on the bags, but they seldom did. The hours we spent counting those little bits of paper mounted up but there was no extra pay for overtime then…

B.G.

I went to work at the fish and chip shop

People used to bring their own paper to wrap up their fish and chips, sometimes we would

Binns Store, Fawcett Street, Sunderland (the fire was caused by incendiary bombs), 10 April 1941.

Cleveland Road, Sunderland bomb damage, 8 April 1941.

Barbara Sowerby outside the fish shop.

get end rolls from the *Echo* [local newspaper]. The servicemen used to come in and if we didn't have any paper they would get all their letters out, put them in their caps, which we filled with fish and chips. I cycled from Hendon to Fulwell, it was cheaper than the tram fare. I paid six pence per week for the bike. It was a hard life cycling back to Hendon at night: because of the blackout I had no lights on the bike. Also as we had to wait for the fat cooling in the pans, it was sometimes one o' clock in the morning.

B.S.

Suddenly we were told y' gannin abroad

We knew there was gonna be a war, like; aal the lads we were mates; so we aal got together,

y' knar, decided we'd aal join the Territorials so we'd aal be together. Better than gett'n caalled up and gett'n sent somewhere and not know'n anybody. I was a shop assistant. Me best mate was a butcher and we aal joined up. We thought we was really soldiers. We got sent on a fortnights trainin' t' Whitby. We just got one week over then somebody declared waar. We had our uniforms and everythin'. Straight away we went back to Dykelands Road. We went t' the Seaburn Centre. It's not there now. We was aal spread out an aah was in the concert haal sleep'n on the floor. Three blankets, that was it like. It was a bit 'ard but y' just gerron wirrit. We got sent aal ower the place sand baggin' along Seaburn 'n that. Suddenly we were told 'y' gannin abroad' an we eventually got sent t' Singapore. In the jungle the guns had been concreted into the ground pointin' out t' sea. The Japs came on bikes behind us! We had no defence. We was captured. Aah worked in the coal-mines and build'n the bridge. When the waar was ower w' came back ower the bridge. We were terrified what would happen, like, 'cause we knew how we had built it!

E.T.

We were not buffoons

In 1941 at the age of seventeen... I joined the Home Guards. On my return to Sunderland that same year, I transferred to Clarks Engineering Works Platoon, under the command of the DLI. Contrary to popular belief we were not the buffoons, as portrayed in *Dads' Army*. We were an efficient fighting force, going on manoeuvres both with and against the regular Army. At the Whitburn Firing Range we fired the rifle, Bren and Sten guns. In the Fulwell quarries we threw grenades and fired the Blaker Bombard and the EY Rifle. In 1944, after three years in the Home Guard, I joined the Army. The only new thing I learned was unarmed combat... to this day I don't think the British Government or the British public really appreciated the Home Guard.

T.H.

The first member of the Southwick Resistance?

I started at Pickies [Pickersgills] in 1939, with stocktakers, aged fourteen. Steel was brought in by horse and cart from Southwick goods yard by contractors Joseph Prior. The primitive toilets were under the jetty overhanging the river. I was in the power house as an apprentice when two Army officers came. Because of possible invasion, plans were laid for the Army to put compressors out of action using me because of my age. Was I the first member of the Southwick Resistance? I had to go into town to Jerome's for my photograph to put in my special Army pass. November 1940, firewatchers were formed - for one night all night per week in case of air-raid fires starting. From the old canteen we moved into the Times Inn outside West Gate Yard.

L.T.

Our Pole had captured his toe

In the 1940s we lived on my grandfather's farm, Seaham Grange, on the outskirts of Sunderland. Early one morning there was a bang and my uncles, Frank and Douglas Davidson, ran outside to see if something was wrong with the tractor. They returned saying there was a parachutist coming down. They grabbed the rifles hanging above the scullery door, and ran out. Baling out of a crashing plane, he shouted, 'Don't shoot! Polish!' Eventually my uncles returned with the limping Polish airman between them. He was taken to the telephone to ring his headquarters. After being given refreshments by Auntie Mary, he gave her a Polish ribbon. A very large service ambulance arrived to take him away. When we went to Byron Terrace School later

that morning, everyone was agog with interest. I told the teacher what had happened and that our Pole had captured his toe, never having heard the word fractured!

V.T.

We just ran wild

The first six months of the war, you didn't have to go to school. We just ran wild. When the schools started up again I remember the teacher coming around the estate to report we had to go to school again. Quite a few of us did a runner to Hylton woods thinking we could stay there all the time, but eventually we had to go back to school again.

L.M.

The place was actually teeming with soldiers

There was a curfew – in fact we wondered why they sent Bede girls to a place like Catterick Camp, because the place was actually teeming with soldiers, especially at weekends and after curfew. We weren't allowed out after five and members of staff had duties parading the town and if you were caught out you were in trouble.

Mrs H.

The education was rather haphazard

All the… villages in Wensleydale had their quota of evacuees from my school. Our schooling was conducted at Askrigg, where we shared the Yorebridge Grammar School with the children from that school. They had the school in the morning, we in the afternoon…The education was rather haphazard for a while until everything settled down, but not for want of trying by our teachers, who were a good bunch and really worked hard, to get the job done.

J.R.

George Brantingham (1914-87) in First World War uniform, but for the Second World War.

Evacuation.

The children had to toe the line

I cannot remember inspecting the houses where the children were put, they were just billeted in any house that was big enough; some of them were big, but contained very old people, which was unsuitable. The children had to toe the line of the house where religion was concerned. Many children had only experienced worshipping in a chapel so being sent to an Anglican church was foreign to them. We used the Methodist Chapel to teach the children their lessons. They liked the choir room best, as it had a gallery and when there was a fire drill they could run round the gallery to the front door. We only paid about £1 per week to the people we were billeted with for all our grub, but again they didn't ever leave us alone in their lounge when going out, we were different and of course we were just Sunderland people weren't we.

M.S.

I was the last one actually

I went to Brompton (about a mile or two out of Northallerton), and assembled in the school hall where there were the members of staff plus all the billet people and we were allocated to our billets one by one. As far as I can recall I think they called out the name of the pupil and then the name of the person they were to be with. They paired up and then disappeared. Then they would read out somebody else's name and they would be paired and leave. I was the last one actually and they didn't have any billets left, so there was a bit of a run around and eventually they found one.

O.T.

We participated in a lot of activities

I had been very keen on the scouts, belonging to the Brompton Beders, which was a breakaway from the Bede pack, and we participated in a lot of activities like scrap paper for the war effort, collecting it and baling it. We also used to, away from the Scouts, go to forestry camps at East Witton in Wensleydale on the hillside, sawing pit props and cutting lower branches off trees so as to help them to fell the trees. That was a voluntary experience.

We also put on a concert, as I remember. One concert was for the residents of Northallerton, which was very popular, and we also did some work in the North Riding County Control for plotting air raids and things. We used to carry messages within the county control from various controllers to others, as a sort of part of the war effort.

O.T.

It was like the switching on of the Christmas lights

When the war ended, one magical evening we children were told to get ready, and the whole family were taken on the bus into the town centre (no cars then). The streets were packed with people, and the whole of the town centre was ablaze with coloured lights. Street lights, neon signs in windows, and to a child after the dark war years it was a sight to remember! I suppose in today's terms, it was like the switching on of the Xmas lights, but so much more effective after the blackout!

S.W.

VE Day street party

On the night, after Churchill had announced the end of the war, a large bonfire was lit nearby and people celebrated late into the night. The blackout had ended a month or more before this. People in the street had been contributing to a street party fund each week for many weeks. A few weeks after VE Day we had a street party with tables and forms from the church positioned end to end in the roadway… There was jelly, flags and bunting hung from the windows. A 'welcome home' banner was hung across the street for any neighbourhood servicemen who were coming home. A piano and gramophone provided the music for dancing.

D.B.

After sixty years…

After sixty years lying buried underground, one of Hitler's bombs was unearthed in Hendon where I live. Just before 5 p.m. on 15 October 2002 the families from our area were told of the situation and that we had to leave our homes. We were evacuated. Some to Southmoor and others to Thornhill school halls. It was only for about a few hours… It turned out to be two days and nights. There was a real threat to our homes, which could have been destroyed all these years after the forgotten bomb was dropped during the Second World War.

M.W.

seven

Working

We sold everything from corn plasters to Cherry Blossom shoe polish

I joined the Co-op in the 1960s during the big clearances in Sunderland. Dilapidated properties (slums) in old parts of the East End and Monkwearmouth were being cleared and the people moved onto huge council housing estates on the edge of town. The houses seemed to be built before the shops and the Co-op was ideally situated to deal with this, they already delivered all over Sunderland. Now they invested in a number of travelling shops to replace the old vans....

We loaded at Green Street every morning. It was very simple. We took aboard what we thought we could sell, then we were invoiced for it. Our takings from the customers was banked every night. It took all of two hours to load up in the old days. Very little was pre-packed. We would weigh out half hundred-weight (56lbs) of butter; sugar; dried fruit etc into packets. The bacon was whole sides sliced and weighed in total. We had one set of scales on the shop, little more than a balance with weights. Eggs were loaded in cardboard boxes of thirty dozen and each two and a half dozen came in a compressed paper tray moulded to the shape of the eggs. Bread was sliced in grease-proof wrappers from Murton Co-op bakery. Cheese, ah! those cheeses, we carried the huge cylindrical cheeses from the cellar, wrapped in linen which was gray-green with mould. We checked them, tearing back the mouldy wrapper to sample a little bit. Cheese never tasted so good. We sold everything from corn-plasters to Cherry Blossom shoe polish; Wills Woodbines to Windowlene.

D.B.

Fenwicks Brewery, Low Row, Sunderland, March 1943.

Left: *Margaret Hudson Brantingham and William Harrison Brantingham.*

Above: *Co-op Society in the 1960s. Dennis Bulmer is in the brown jacket.*

everything in those days that could be scooped on the scales. Vegetables were weighed on separate scales using cast iron or brass weights.

C.B.

Most of it… we had to put up into bags

There was tinned food and breakfast cereals… Most of it, the likes of sugar, we had to put up into bags. Sugar had blue one pound bags. Butter we used to have to put up into half pounds, quarter pounds and sometimes even two ounce pats, depending – because when I first started there was still food rationing. There was a lot of things needed a ration book and you used to have to either cut out the little coupons or put a mark through them. The senior assistant sliced the bacon and cooked meats or sometimes the manager did it.

Biscuits usually came in large square tins about a cubic twelve inches and they were displayed while still in the tins on a special rack of shelves. In the interests of hygiene the tin lids were replaced with Perspex covers so the customer could see the contents. You weighed nearly

Our place of work burnt to the ground

One of my most vivid memories, (even though it was over fifty years ago), was when I worked in the shoe department of Jopling's here in Sunderland. It was Christmas time, Tuesday 14 December 1954. That morning, as usual, I boarded the circle route tramcar at Millfield, to take me to the terminus outside the railway station in High Street. I met up with some of my friends and we walked together, laughing and chatting. We were planning our Christmas Eve celebrations and deciding whether to go to The Rink or maybe the Seaburn Hall.

Our chattering soon came to an abrupt ending as we saw, to our horror, our place of work burnt to the ground. Only the girders were still standing and smoke was rising up from this sad sight. Only the day before we had all been going happily about our business. Luckily no one was hurt in the fire and Jopling's soon opened for business again.

Girls from Jopling's shoe department.

A temporary store was put up on the old site whilst a new store was built in John Street. It opened for business in May 1956.

L.C.

One day I was asked to wear a real fur coat

My first job was in Binns: I was junior on the mantle and gown department. One day I was asked to wear a real fur coat. This was because a man from the *Echo* was coming to draw this coat to advertise it on the front page of the paper. Binn's always had this spot. This was how advertisements were done. No photography then. After this sketch was done me dad always called me a Binns Model.

M.H.

I started work in Jopling's temporary store

I started work in Jopling's temporary store in 1955. It was built on the site of the old store that was burnt down in the fire the year before. A brand new store was being built in John Street. and we were all very excited about moving in. I was in the shoe department and we spent weeks packing boxes and loading them on to the back of the trucks. Off we went to the new store and got everything ready for opening day. We all had new black dresses which cost 29s 11d and we really thought we were the bees knees. Jopling's was a lovely store and holds a special place in my heart. That was fifty-two years ago and I'm still friends with some of the girls I worked with: they were such happy days.

A.H.

THE shop

In 1920 my father was manager of Hills Bookshop, which was THE shop. They supplied the shipping firms with stationery to keep the accounts in. Hills also supplied the subscription library, which was in Fawcett Street. You paid a pound to be a member.

Choose from the finest furs at Binns. 21 December, 1951, from the Sunderland Echo.

When you went you could get all sorts of stories and all sorts of books. They supplied schools. They supplied the Church High School, then sent the bill to the parents.

Miss B.

My great-granddad had a furniture shop

Francis McGuinness was my great-granddad, he had a furniture shop down the High Street near the Arcade and the Market. He went blind and would sit outside his door and talk to passers-by till he was in his eighties. In the market was lots of stalls – clothes stalls, a bruised fruit stall where you got a halfpenny bag. You could get a butcher's 'wrap-up' for a shilling – sausage and the likes, bits and pieces. Buy prams from Palmers, bikes, and sweet stalls. A rig-out for six pence. Furnish houses with second-hand furniture bought off me great granddad. He was well known. He would sell his own whisky for a half crown. His sons done time for selling the whisky, Steven and Fred, and fined. They got caught 'cause they left the fire on under the still.

E.B.

We had a second-hand furniture business

We had the second-hand furniture business. I've seen me when business was slack, if anybody came into the shop and fancied a bedroom suite and we hadn't one in I've taken them in me bedroom and sold them me full furniture. So anyway this couple wanted a bedroom suite because they were getting married. We had nothing to suit them. I said 'I've a nice one upstairs.' I took them up and they fancied it and took the lot away. I was pregnant and I wasn't long in having to have me baby. I wanted a beautiful bedroom for when the doctor came in… During the night I took me pains. Our Albie and me husband had to carry an ordinary dressing table and an old bed. So I had a shabby bedroom when the doctor came.

S.N.

My husband took over the cat meat business

Me husband took over the cat meat business when his father died. Slaughtering horses. If a horse fell in the street and broke his leg well of

Vaux drays, 1900.

course you had to go out and kill them. When pit ponies were old, you know: instead of giving them to people, they used to get them slaughtered. We had a licence from the colliery here and Ryhope right up to Blackhall. All this side of the North if they didn't bring the ponies to us we would go out with our horse and get them.

S.N.

The word was soon passed around the streets

Men came round with their baskets of wet fish for sale. When the ships used to dock, there were these men more like Indians (of course we were not used to seeing them then), they had these big travelling cases full with goods such as silk scarfs, hankies and clothing.

They were a bit frightening when they used to knock on the door, the case was opened for viewing and mothers could never get rid of them. If anyone of them was seen coming along the word was soon passed around the street so the doors never were opened.

G.A.

I was a female beer taster

For thirty years I was a female beer taster at Vaux Brewery until it closed in 1999. Never actually swallowed the beer, but fumes from the early open vats could make you feel pretty woozy. Later on closed vats were installed and not long after that the business was closed by the London-based consortium of shareholders and the whole site was demolished.

C.

I was a foyboatman for thirty years

I served my time as a cabinet maker, but left the trade in 1947 to join my family tradition as a foyboatman on our famous river Wear. My ancestors and family have been boatmen going back to the eighteen hundreds. The river Wear was one of the largest shipbuilding rivers in the world with seven dry-docks, ten shipyards, thirty pilots, thirty foyboatmen and fourteen tug boats. I was a foyboatman for thirty years; also I repaired the Foyboats in my workshop at North Dock where there was Blumer's Shipyard, Donkin's Scrapyard and Armstrong Addison's Timber Yard. When I go over our famous Wearmouth Bridge and see no ships, it is very sad as I have seen our river full of new ships and colliers waiting to load coal.

G.H.D.

Keeping the scotch glue hot

I started as a floor boy, making teas, keeping the scotch glue hot at Coutts Findlater Shopfitters, Hendon. My first job, a 12in by 12in mirror into a wood frame, fix it with beads and pins. The worst thing could happen did. I cracked the mirror. Mr Coutts (Scotchman called Sandy) was informed. He made a beeline for my bench and got a clout across the ear, 'you will have to put your coat on and go home lad'. Then he said, 'where are you going?' I said, 'You told me to go home', he said, 'What will your mam, say'

'She's dead, Mr Coutts.' Then he said, 'Your father, what is he going to say?'

'My father is dead also.'

'Who is looking after you?'

'My aunt, Mr Coutts.'

'Ay lad. Get back on your bench and take your coat off'. I finished my apprenticeship in 1938 when I was twenty-one. First wage 4s 6d a week, now 35s.

L.R.D.

At the Rectory Sweet Factory

After leaving school at the age of fourteen, I was given a job at the Rectory Sweet Factory, that was in Paley Street, beside the Sunderland Empire Theatre. The managers name was a Mr Walton Bell, who was middle aged then, but a real nice manager. They mainly made boiled sweets, but on occasions made soft-centre boiled sweets like mint humbugs, and soft centre fruits. My first job was to boil up the sugar in a huge copper pan till the sugar was melted then add the colouring and the flavouring. Then the big boys took over to pour it onto the cooling slab to be teased and pulled and dragged to the size required along to the long table, where the other girls were rolling pressing and chopping it into the required shapes, and then wrapping all by hand. The loose sweets were put into glass jars and the wrapped ones put into boxes, and then stored till the van came and took them to all the local shops in Sunderland.

A.E.

Pupil teaching

When I started teaching, [and] when my sister started, they had to go a week to the school that they were appointed to, that was your teaching practice, then a week to a place attached there, the pupil-teacher centre, but by the time I got there, that had been taken into the Bede School, so we had to go. Well I started pupil teaching at Southwick in the August, then the next Easter I had to go to the Bede for a year and then we had to start studying again and then we took the Senior Oxford Exam – nine subjects.

Miss B.

Good wages in the post-war years

I continued in education and eventually qualified as a teacher. Inevitably most of my later teens were spent in the penury of student life, so in that sense I am less typical of my generation. Many of my friends who were working were earning comparatively good wages in the post-war years. Many of the boys in our group became apprentices in the shipbuilding or engineering trades and most joined the Merchant Navy at the age of eighteen.

A.M.

To dress in casual clothing...

As that time teachers and even aspiring teachers were expected to dress quite formally, in smart suits or dresses. To dress in casual clothing would have been frowned on by the head teacher and then goodbye to any prospect of promotion.

A.M.

You look like a nurse

I remember the time it was during the war, I was seventeen years old, and it was 1941. A chance remark by my mother; 'you look like a nurse'. I was wearing my navy coat and white shirt; my reply was, 'I wish I was'. This prompted me to write to the matron at the Royal Infirmary. After being granted an interview, I was accepted as a student nurse. Probation was three months. At the end of three months, if accepted and deciding to continue, you were paid. Otherwise you had worked three months without pay. At the time we had one day off per calendar month. First year salary £1 10s a month. After four years I completed my nurse training and was accepted into general nursing at the Sunderland Royal Infirmary.

J.W.

A very busy place

I lived near the Sunderland Fish Quay in the 1930s-40s, which was a very busy place because of the ferry, which went across the river to Monkwearmouth. The fisherwomen, who had strong minds and who were physically strong as they lived hard lives, would be familiar figures on the quayside. They would twist an old towel and wrap it round their head to carry the baskets: they were quite graceful as well. My daughter sold fish, she would pay five pence on the ferry to the Blockyard, which was a saw mill, and she had bought some herring and kippers or whatever which she sold by walking up and down the streets of Monkwearmouth shouting and folk would come out with their dishes to put the fish on. My husband's grandmother was a fisherwoman, she was as tough as an old boot, she would buy broken kippers from the Kipper Warehouse and sew them together and sell them as a whole pair of kippers. People going to the beach used the ferry, and the fishermen were coming and going. Flowers Brewery and the shipyards were by it. The shipyards were a way of life as they used to wake you up at 7.30 a.m. with the hooters so no one slept in, also it went at 12 noon.

W.D.

A dangerous place to work

I... went to Bartram's shipyard sweeping up and making tea for buttons until I was sixteen and began as a shipwright apprentice. I began work at 7 a.m. and lost an hour's pay if I was five minutes late... At one time a welder wanted his break from the deck, so he wedged a metal sleeve on a vertical pipe instead of welding it. I was in the engine room and grasped the base of the pipe. The sleeve came loose, slid down and sliced off the top of my finger. I got £250 compensation but it remained a dangerous place to work. Cotton wool was the only protection from all the noise. There was strict demarcation of work. Once when the welder was missing I picked

Herring Drifters, south dock, Sunderland, 1951.

A broadside launch at Robert Thompson's Bridge Dockyard, Sunderland.

Austin Pickergill Shipyard in Sunderland.

up a chance to weld a small job so I could get on. The foreman and the shop steward nearly paid me off for that. Although I was twice awarded Best Apprentice of the Year, I was only kept on for a year after passing my apprenticeship and was then paid off to 'get worldly experience'.

J.R.P.

The largest marine engine

I worked for George Clark NE Marine in the 1950s, as an engineering fitter. They were based in Southwick on the north side of Alexander Bridge. They built marine engines... The foreman always wanted us to speed up jobs, but quality was the priority. The tolerances between parts were more for sewing machines than ship engines. Clarks employed all trades and had the largest crane operating in the town. They closed down in 1972; the jobs transferred to Newcastle. I remember the Lloyds Register examiner saying, 'With Doxford's know how and Clark's finish they have a real world beater.'

D.W.

My first job was to pound lumps of coloured glass

On leaving school I started work at Hartley Wood glassworks. My first job was to pound lumps of coloured glass to the size of a pea. Saturday morning was for wheeling coke in for the furnaces. A short time later I began to work with a qualified glass blower learning to blow window glass, mainly coloured for churches etc. The blower would collect the glass from the furnace with his rod and proceed to shape it with pair of tongs: when he got the shape he wanted he passed the rod with the softened glass on for me to blow steadily. When it reached the required dimension he would knock the glass off onto a conveyer belt that went through the kiln for cooling down the process at the other end. A glass cutter would cut both ends then length-wise down the middle. It was dipped in the cold water and sent to another furnace where the glass started to open out. A man with a long handled rod with a pad on the end smoothed and flattened the glass which was cooled once again, then moved along a belt where the glass cutter with his T-square would cut it and put it into the racks.

G.G.

Craven's Angels

When I was fifteen I went to work as office girl at British Ropes in Roker Avenue, and I have lots of happy memories of the place, particularly of the factory girls, Craven's Angels. I saw a lot of them because most of my first year and a half was spent taking endless pieces of paper down into the works, and searching for the right person to give them to.

My clearest memory is of the Cord Mill, which was the high building covered in white tiles which you came to first when coming down Roker Avenue. I remember as if it was yesterday climbing the steps to the top floor. The noise from the machinery was tremendous, and the clattering and rattling scared the life out of me the first time I went in. The girls all had knives dangling from their waists on pieces of twine and they couldn't speak, they just had to hoot and point when they tried to tell me where the works manager was, or whoever my message was for.

The thing that made the most impression on me though was the hemp dust; it was floating about all over the place, falling thick on the stairs in the girls' hair and on their eyelashes. To me – no doubt not to them, although they seemed happy enough – it was a memory I will never forget.

J.G.

Austin Pickergill Shipyard, Sunderland.

Doxford Shipyard, Sunderland.

Websters Ropery. (R. Wear, Sunderland)

There were six generations of Moons on the tugboats

As ar say there were six generations of 'Moons' on the tugboats and when they finally came to an end was a very, very sad occasion... Me grandfather wouldn't allow me father to go on the tugs, so that's how he became a blacksmith. Truly and simply it was because the wage structure wasn't there, so me father missed it. Y'know, what was the good of you following in our footsteps when you are not going to get the pay? So me father missed it and when ar said ar was going on, he wasn't best pleased that ar wanted to serve. Even though there wasn't an official apprenticeship, you had to serve four years on the boats, then – y'know – you sort of became a 'man' if you like. So it was, opinions change. When he found out ar was earning three times more than him – my God!

G.M.

The tugboat Cornhill.

A fitting memorial

In 1933-35 my father Thomas Taylor was in charge of the demolition of the Holey Rock at Roker and the building of the sea wall from Roker Park to the Cat and Dog Steps. It was indeed a Trojan task, because he and his workmen had to contend with heavy seas. In the beginning of the wall building, two men were killed when the gantry collapsed due to rough seas and work had to be started again... The rough seas constantly pounding would dislodge the wall... Whenever I go down to the Cat and Dog Steps I remember the two men who died.

O.H.

Two very important people

Two very important people did their night walks. The lamp lighter saw that all the gas lamps were lit. The lamp-posts were made of

Roker Sands, 1900.

cast iron with a glass top arrangement, which held the gas fittings and the mantle. He had a long pole with a hook on the end, also a little paraffin lamp. He would place this in the case at the top, connecting the hook to a lever which would turn on the gas, also the light. He would return in the early hours and turn the lights off. The second was the Caller. People… used to pay this person to knock on windows so they would not oversleep and be late for work.

T.H.

Operator, are you on the line?

In 1953 I joined the workers in Telephone House as a 'hello girl'. Mind this was a misnomer, we always had to say 'number please' and the strict supervisors made sure we did. The girls' shifts covered 8 a.m. to 6 p.m. weekdays, and then the men took over at the switchboard panels. All calls were recorded on tickets, col-

lected by the supervisors. Actually no bells rang, lights flashed – a red one with a buzzer for emergencies. Reporters and bookmakers made Saturdays busy, as well as some heavy breathing freaks and daft lad's with 'Operator, are you on the line? Well, gerroff. There's a train coming!' Pay was good at £7 10s a week including times of sickness and everyone was happy and friendly.

M.M.

We would open the boxes on the toilet doors

I left school in 1940 and the head mistress sent me to the borough treasurer's office, Town Hall, Fawcett Street to commence work in the Wages Department. I did not have to fill in an application form or sign anything. All the wages were in pounds, shillings and pence and put into brown envelopes. Every Friday these envelopes were placed on a tray, open

The joiners shop in Austin's.

for anyone to pick off, but no one did, then by taxi I went to the Transport Depot at the top of Silksworth Row Bank to dish out the wages. I was only a junior at the time. Another task was, a senior lady and myself, would go each week to the underground Victorian Public convenience at Seaburn. With a key we would open the boxes on the toilet doors to collect and count the pennies.

A.R.

For two years it was just great

I left Grange Park School in 1947 when I was fourteen. There were plans for me to go into Thompson's shipyard to be an apprentice pattern maker but I couldn't start until I was sixteen. So the personnel officer, Mr Gardener, asked me to go to Belford House in Ashbrooke to work in their wonderful big gardens with Mr Charlton. For two years it was just great for sixteen shillings and five pence a week. Then I was sixteen. After only two days in the busy, noisy shipyards I was back at Sir Norman and Lady Thompson's gardens, but six months later I was called insolent for asking for a rise to match the Park's wages and had to leave. I went to work my way up in the Authority Parks and Cemeteries for forty-four years. The saddest thing was in 2006 – empty Belford House was attacked by arsonists and the beautiful wooden staircases and fireplaces were destroyed.

R.W.

There was a restriction then you know

I started work at the Central Laundry at fourteen. I lived in Maud Street and me mam paid 21s 6d a week rent. I worked in the Central till I was sixteen, it was in Fullwell. When you got to sixteen I was paid off. One Christmas time we had to work overtime, there was a restriction then, you know. I started work at eight o'clock. We worked till half past nine at night.

And worked till four o'clock on a Saturday and I was thrilled to bits with my wages, I got a ten shilling note and a threepenny bit, a silver threepenny bit. I started at 3s 6d then rose to 7s 6d a week.

P.W.

Putt'n was one of the hardest jobs in the pit…

The putter was the lad, or it could be the man, that actually put the tub from where it was filled out to the landen. But putt'n was one of the hardest jobs in the pit… In some places… the tub could barely travel because the roadway was only the height of the tub and of course again you come back to the gallower, if you've got a good gallower, it wasn't so bad, but if you got a bad gallower and you kept getting off the way… you could have a tough shift and earn no money and it was back brick'n work… When the tub dropped off the way, they had to be lifted manually. At Silksworth they were ten hundred weight and when they got the steel tubs, they reckon up to eleven hundred weight so you had a man trying to lift half a ton back on the way…

W.C.

The pit was the heart of the colliery village

Why, the pit was the most important thing in the village, everything revolved around the pit and the Co-operative Store; if you wanted a box of matches you had to go reet down to the store to get a box of matches. The Co-operative man used to come round and take his order on his lang list and the groceries were delivered to y' door. But the pit y'know was the heart of the colliery village. Ya negotiated the time by the buzzer, the buzzer used to go at certain intervals and you knew exactly what time it was. It was also the sound

Monkwearmouth Colliery,
Sunderland, 1982.

Second Durham miners' gala,
1930s.

everybody dreaded when somebody was killed at the pit, because it used to repeat y' know, repeat short blasts on the buzzer, everybody knew that somebody'd been killed.

W.C.

Oh they had to be seriously injured

I can remember one time there was only me and my brother in the house and the ambulance brought me father (a miner) to the door, black and he'd had both his fingers bursted wide open… The doctor come and tended to him and his fingers turned septic, mind they were split wide open and the nurse or doctor put blue-stone on to burn the poison out; and the poor bugger he had to walk the floor for twenty-four hours y'know with this stuff on his fingers… and his fingers at the end were deformed. Oh they had to be seriously injured before they took them into hospital.

W.C.

We had to stand shoulder to shoulder

As a policeman I was dismayed at colleagues who treated the striking miners with unnecessary violence. A few of us in the station did a collection for one nice family who were really hit hard. Officers from outside the area were brought in. Sometimes bricks were flying round and people going down. We had to stand shoulder to shoulder.

J.V.

The Sunderland rat catcher

The Sunderland rat catcher was my dad. His name was Patrick Carroll, and we all lived together in 4 Woodbine Street in the east end of Sunderland near to the Dock Hotel pub... Very often when we were having our meals, me and my brothers and sisters would be eating our meals, with rats that was running about in metal cages under the table... He

would often leave lying around the house bags of dead rats, that he had caught on his rounds. He would put all his dead rats in one bag and then set off to take them to the health office that was then situated in Thornholme Road to be disposed of. I used to think that he kept those live rats to let loose near to premises to make the owner think that they had rats.

T.P.

I can tell you a lot about what the washerwomen did...

I was born at Hallgarth Square baths and washhouses in 1924, and I think I can tell you a lot about what the washerwomen did. Some ladies came in everyday because they took in washing for half a crown a time and when you came to the office my mother used to give you a ticket for three ha'pence an hour, so it all depended on how many hours you wanted to stop in, but on top of that you got a penn'worth of soap, ha' penny of soda, a penny carbostle and a penny blue bag, that was to keep your whites white. Every person had an individual stand that consisted of a rinsing basin, a hot basin, a tub, and a poss stick, they used to wear great big coarse aprons and men's boots because there was a lot of water about, you see, when they emptied the tubs.

There was also a drying house, that was under the big boiler from the fireman's hut, where there were great big stands, clothes horses, one up and one down and they were all on pulleys, and you pulled them out, they were all numbered so what ever your clothes went on, you numbered it, and they hung there till they dried or maybe they would go home and come back to collect them... Then they would go up into the mangling room with the great big mangles where they mangled the sheets.

There were two rows of baths on the other side of the building and the first set was threepence per person, which included a

The rat catcher.

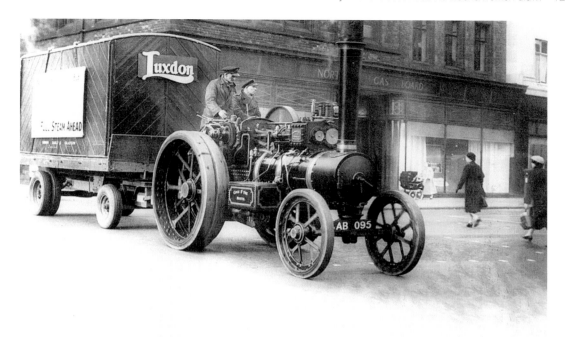

Luxdon laundry van, Sunderland, 1958.

Monkwearmouth Colliery trip to Knaresboro, 15 July 1964.

Lambton Staiths, Sunderland, 1960s.

Jennings Foundry, Sunderland.

Pyrex.

towel. When the shipyards were quite busy we used to get a lot of people in, but when the work finished they could come in for three ha' pence per bath and we did have quite a few people coming in.

J.C.

But your marrer at the pit…

Your marrer at the pit was the man that you worked with. In lots of cases it was father and son, other times it was by choice and that was you' marrer, the man you work with. Now they used to be in sets, now they used to be a set of six men, so they were you' marrers the whole lot although they would be in different shifts. In fact I've seen that there's been twenty-five to twenty-six men and they've been classed as marrers and at the end of the quarter, especially in big sets like that if they thought some of the men weren't pulling their weight, they used to tell them, 'now at the end of the quarter find yourself fresh marrers…'

W.C.

Hand fill'n

Now after the machine had cut the coal and the coal was fired down, men used to go on the face with shovels; again the sets could be used as far as sets of six, sets of twelve or as many as twenty odd and they used to go on with shovels, picks, saws and fill the coal and timmer the face up as they filled the coal off. And you can imagine if the face was a couple of hundred yards long or 180 yards long to get in the middle of that face, you would have to creep about ninety yards and that ninety yards you had to creep was, it would be about a yard or under, you would have to creep across the fired coal, so you were dragging a shovel, pick, saw, possibly an oil lamp you' bait, you' bottle and anywhere, a foot, eighteen inches high across coal that had just been fired, it was like having to creep across barbed wire at times, that's just to get to the place you worked… Now the prices you paid for such work was disgusting, men literally had to kill themselves to get a liv'n' wage.

W.C.

Zelda the headless lady

In the fifties I worked at the fairground at Seaburn. It was my first job to sit in the little box, take the entrance money and give out the tickets. Then while Mr Hillard tore the ticket in half and shoved them in a dark place at the back of the show I ran around and stepped into the magic box. I was Zelda the headless lady who could see all and hear all… I had travelled from home in Preston in answer to an advertisement in the stage newspaper. Mr Hillard wanted a show girl for his side shows at Seaburn… I was in the sideshow from ten in the morning to ten at night. It was a long summer, bed to work. This didn't put me off Sunderland – this is still my home.

K.C.F.

Other local titles published by The History Press

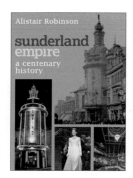

Sunderland Empire: A Centenary History

ALISTAIR ROBINSON

One hundred years of entertainment at Sunderland Empire is celebrated in 2007 and this lavishly illustrated history tells its story. From the glory days of the Edwardian Music Hall to the high-tech glamour of *Starlight Expressz* the theatre has remained an important part of Sunderland's history through the twentieth century and now, following a lavish refurbishment, continues into the twenty-first as the premier centre for entertainment in the area.

978 0 7524 4340 9

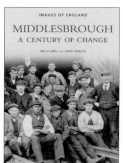

Middlesbrough: A Century of Change

IAN STUBBS AND JENNY PARKER

This splendid selection of over 270 old photographs of Middlesbrough illustrates some of the many changes that have occurred in the town over the twentieth century. These nostalgic images show the town and its buildings over those years; its streets, transport, industries, churches and houses. They also show the people at work and play; in factories, schools and at leisure, playing sport or watching celebratory events.

978 0 7524 3720 0

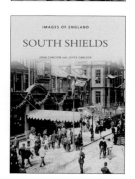

South Shields

JOHN CARLSON AND JOYCE CARLSON

Once a hub of the ship-building and coal-mining trades, South Shields has witnessed the full-scale demise of these industries and has had to adjust to new businesses, including promoting itself as a small seaside resort. This fascinating selection of more than 190 images illustrates some of the changes that South Shields has seen over the years and is sure to evoke nostalgic memories for those who worked or lived in the town in its industrial heyday and will be a revelation for newcomers and for those to young to remember.

978 0 7524 4077 4

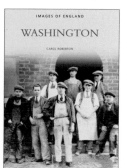

Washington

CAROL ROBERTON

The medieval manor of Washington gave its name to the family of President George Washington and through him, to the capital of the United States of America. Locals here proudly claim to be the 'original Washington'! Using a fascinating selection of old photographs Carol Roberton tells the story of the Old Hall, ancestral home of the Washington family, and the village, and traces the development and industrialisation of the surrounding villages which now form part of Washington New Town in the city of Sunderland.

978 0 7524 4000 2

If you are interested in purchasing other books published by The History Press, or in case you have difficulty finding any of our books in your local bookshop, you can also place orders directly through our website

www.thehistorypress.co.uk